1995

THE FAMILY IN THE AGE OF BIOTECHNOLOGY

The Society for Applied Philosophy is concerned with the philosophical discussion of areas of practical concern, including environmental and medical ethics, the social implications of scientific and technical change, and philosophical and ethical issues in education, law and economics.

Membership enquiries to:

The Honorary Secretary Ms Jane Pritchard
Centre for Professional Ethics
University of Central Lancashire
Preston PR1 2HE

The Family in the Age of Biotechnology

CAROLE ULANOWSKY
School of Health and Social Welfare
The Open University

Avebury

Aldershot · Brookfield USA · Hong Kong · Singapore · Sydney

© C.E. Ulanowsky 1995

© Chapter 9 P. Gregory 1995

Published by
Avebury
Ashgate Publishing Limited
Gower House
Croft Road
Aldershot
Hants GU11 3HR
England

Ashgate Publishing Company
Old Post Road
Brookfield
Vermont 05036
USA

British Library Cataloguing in Publication Data

Family in the Age of Biotechnology
I. Ulanowsky, Carole
176

ISBN 1 85628 955 9

Library of Congress Catalog Card Number: 94-73709

Printed in Great Britain by Ipswich Book Co. Ltd., Ipswich, Suffolk.

Contents

v

List of contributors

Brenda Almond is Professor of Moral and Social Philosophy at the University of Hull. She is Chair of the Society for Applied Philosophy and Joint Editor of the Journal of Applied Philosophy. Her books include *Moral Concerns and Exploring Philosophy*.

Bob Brecher is Principal Lecturer in Philosophy in the School of Historical and Critical Studies at the University of Brighton. Publications include *Anselm's argument: The Logic of Divine Existence* plus articles in *Journal of Medical Ethics, Radical Philosophy, Philosophy* and in various collections. Main interests are in moral philosophy and currently working on *A Critique of Liberal Morality*.

Phillip Cole is Senior Lecturer in Applied Philosophy at Middlesex University where he is also a member of The Centre for Practical Philosophy. His research interests are citizenship, welfare and social justice. Phillip Cole has published in *The Journal of Applied Philosophy* and other collections. He is currently preparing a book on *Liberty and Social Justice*.

Paul Gregory graduated from the University of Kent at Canterbury in 1974. He has lived mainly in Germany, where he is now a freelance translator and interpreter in Hamburg. He has published a number of philosophical articles on the nature of love and sexuality, and also has an interest in business ethics.

Neil Leighton worked for many years as a social worker in particular with children and families. He progressed to senior management but, following early retirement, was recycled back into specialist practice with children involved in court proceedings. A regular contributor to professional journals, Neil now has an interest in the ethics of social work in particular "rights and responsibilities" and the ethical issues around state interventions.

Sandra E Marshall teaches in the Philosophy Department at the University of Stirling. She has written a number of articles in the area of medical ethics and legal and social philosophy.

Neil Pickering is a University College Fellow in the Centre for Philosophy and Health Care, University College, Swansea. His research includes work on moral arguments concerning infertility treatment and the moral status of the human embryo.

Marilyn Strathern is Professor of Social Anthropology at the University of Cambridge. Current research interests include gender, kinship and the new reproductive technologies.

Martin Thomasson is a Lecturer in Philosophy at Bolton Institute of Higher Education. His research interests are in philosophy of human personal relationships and in environmental philosophy.

Steve Wilkinson is Lecturer in Philosophy at the University of Keele. His research interests include moral theory and applied ethics, rationality and motivation, epistemology and the philosophy of science.

Acknowledgements

Grateful thanks to Jenny Skidmore for assistance with preparing this
manuscript and to Beryl Unway for assistance with proofreading.

For my children

Introduction

In 1978, with the birth of the first ever test-tube baby, a milestone was reached in reproductive technology. Now, women of pensionable age can become mothers, preferences of race, even of gender for one's progeny can be realized, and it is technically possible for a person to be created from the ova of an aborted fetus - a living child from a never-living mother. These advances introduce biological complexities into an already ethically charged landscape for the family. With a current UK. statistic of one marriage in three ending in divorce, it is the case that many will live long term in a "family" setting, but with people who are not biologically related to them. So, whilst there is an urgent call for debate when the laboratory impinges upon family relationships, as with biotechnology, the case is strong too for a more holistic appraisal of the settings and structures for procreation and nurture which are already apparent in society, as of those we might anticipate for the future. This volume offers a contribution to that appraisal.

From a variety of perspectives, these writers tease out the critical elements from a landscape affected by sociological change as well as by technological advance. These critical elements include "fulfilment" and "choice" and "rights" and "responsibilities" as well as the question of bonding and kinship within the new environments. This is with a recognition that, whilst the changes which are upon us through scientific advance have not been around long enough for us to appraise their likely implications, neither too have the new familial connections been tested over time. However, change and advance are part of the dynamic of human existence. The problem here is to try to establish which changes are likely to increase possibilities for human fulfilment and which changes are unlikely to do so; critically, to take steps to ensure that "change", whether biological or sociological, does not bequeath problems for future generations to solve.

1

Compiled during The International Year of The Family, mostly from papers presented at The Society for Applied Philosophy's annual conference, this volume will be of interest to a broad range of professionals. In particular, it will interest those who recognise, for the sake of future generations, the importance of proceeding appropriately at this present time. There are contentious issues within the family debate, and the ten contributors engage with these issues from a variety of perspectives. At all times, they write as individuals.

Biotechnology: Demands and controls

Currently, around one in six couples in the UK. experiences infertility problems. Scientists look to environmental reasons to explain the ever lower sperm counts in men; for women, the reasons are various but might include an increasing incidence of those sexually transmitted diseases which attack the reproductive function; another factor could be the postponement of first pregnancy beyond the years of highest fertility. Clearly, whatever the cause, the very real anguish experienced by people unable to realize their reproductive potential argues for solutions to be found and consequently for ever increasing demands upon fertility services. The publicity around new "breakthroughs" can create an optimism not borne out through evidence, however, as the overall success rate for live babies of, for example, in vitro fertilisation(IVF), is currently not more than 15%.

Additionally, with a Health Service needing to balance ever more competing demands at a time of stringent audit, the issue of who gets what, and who decides, is never far away. This "resources and rights" problem introduces a further dimension to the ethical debate which lies at the very heart of these scientific advances.

It appears to be the case that there is something especially problematic with advances in the reproductive area of medicine, extra to the natural aversion initially registered with, say, the first donated heart, or kidney. For where *potential* as opposed to *actual* life is at issue, scientific intervention can sometimes be viewed as "scientists playing God". Yet, on the other side, it can be said that, through biotechnology, scientists are not creating matter, merely *manipulating* it, for only God can create something from nothing...

It is undeniably the case that the use of donated sperm, eggs and embryos is becoming part of our reproductive environment, as is surrogacy and fertilisation in the laboratory, through IVF. However, the incidence of other techniques, both actual and potential, for example, ectogenesis - the development of embryos in artificial wombs - and the possibility for male pregnancies, present an image of conception and birth fundamentally

2

detached from our previous understandings of these. With advances moving apace, The Human Fertilisation and Embryology Authority was established in the 1980s to regulate assisted reproduction and, in 1990, The Human Fertilization and Embryology Act, provided legislation to govern the manipulation of new life outside the body.

Areas of concern

"Will the test-tube baby be happy?" A newspaper headline from a decade ago seems prophetic in the light of current concerns as the separation of biological from legal and social parenthood becomes more and more of a reality. As Marilyn Strathern in *New Families for Old* points out, biotechnology has initiated not just *biological* change, but fundamental changes at the heart of people's understanding - in the way they actually *think* about reproduction and parenthood. So with a growing potential for the laboratory to impinge ever more on human futures there is call for reflective space. However, the current rate of scientific advance means that ethicists and legislators will hardly be afforded that space.

As indicated earlier in this introduction, it is not just the new technologies which are challenging time-honoured views of parenthood and the family, but society itself. For whilst there is a growing recognition on the part of those who push science to its limits that they ought not to bequeath problems for the future to solve, so too must those who have a part to play in the begetting and rearing of children through natural means, have a similar concern through the settings *they* create and sustain. The broader question then has to be, "Will the *child* be happy?" Drawing upon anthropological, social and legal as well as philosophical perspectives, this book attempts to address this issue of settings for the begetting and rearing of children. It is perhaps no exaggeration to claim that the family is an area which can present particular philosophical problems, not only because the attendant issues are complex and cover a broad landscape, but because, as will be seen in these papers, good and bad arguments are frequently evenly matched. Additionally, some feel that to begin the debate from a baseline of traditional understandings of the family is probably misconstrued when, in society, these are already subject to serious challenge.

Power and patriarchy

Some writers in this volume believe that the new birth technologies hold the promise of deconstructing traditional ways of thinking about the family.

They envisage the nuclear family, with mother and father caring for their own biological children, as a thing of the past, as state and society adopt more flexible approaches to procreative and care structures; this notion might be expressed not just attitudinally but in legislative and economic terms. Phillip Cole, in Chapter 3 says that he was initially hopeful that, through biotechnology, "the social and biological structures of the family would come apart". However, he notes that currently this new state of affairs is not being allowed to "take its course" due to "discriminatory state interventions". As Cole interprets it, new Bodies with new legislation, monitor and control the new technologies; thus there is greater control over who shall and shall not become parents than has been the case to date with natural, biological parenting. Cole believes that the 1990 Human Fertilisation and Embryology Act, bears all the hall marks of a "pro-familist ideology" in its call for a screening system for all prospective parents: by implication, Cole claims, children produced through fertility treatment are seen as "at risk" if not parented within traditional nuclear structures. Cole concludes from this that, whilst through new technologies relationships might have the potential to be radically new, the frameworks of control mean that traditional family structures will be preserved; whilst some can see the obvious wisdom of this, it is not a state of affairs he would welcome. This "outrageous prejudice", he claims, is perpetrated not just on moral, but on economic grounds and he draws an analogy with wider Government policies to restrict fatherless and less-controlled family forms, through the benefits system.

Sandra Marshall in her chapter *Choosing the Family* also has something to say on the matter of reproductive technology doled out on the grounds of political expediency and Marilyn Strathern in Chapter 2, notes that biotechnology could lend support to the old patriarchies. In some ways, these authors tell us, those who develop the technologies as those who apportion them, may be inclined to operate their own agendas.

A tripartite division

Changes in society over the past twenty years or so, observable, for example, through the increasing incidence of reconstituted families linked to high divorce rates and breakdown of relationships, in real terms demonstrate a separation of the different aspects of parenthood - biological, legal and functional (in contrast with the *whole* experience of traditional nuclear families where two biological parents raise, to adulthood, their own shared offspring). For example, a father, involved in a second relationship, may become the caring/social parent of his partner's offspring whilst giving little

4

or no input to the bringing up of his own, biological, offspring. It is the case that the new birth technologies could open the door to increased opportunities for this tripartite division. This is a subject looked at in some detail by Brenda Almond in the opening chapter *Family Relationships and Reproductive Technology*. Almond registers her concern about this fragmentation and reminds us that the new technologies open up a whole new age of "relationships by choice" which, whilst in some ways to be welcomed, is by no means unproblematic. On the issue of *social* parenthood (the holding of parental responsibility), as against *biological* parenthood, she looks at recent legislation and notes a continuing bias in favour of biological ties, but remarks that this is unwelcome to some who prefer to interpret the apparently "natural" in parent/child relations as "socially engineered". In this regard, Almond takes a critical look at the legal theorist, Eekelaar, who says:

> All attributes of parenthood are social... so the choice is not between "social engineering and following nature" - but between different kinds of social engineering.

For this and other reasons, Eekelaar would shift the duty of care, whatever the context of procreation, to the state, and this radical view is supported by some other writers in this volume.

Kith and kin

Whilst Marilyn Strathern notes her concern about justice and equity in relation to policies around the "new technologies and families" which appear to favour *traditional* models, in her chapter she registers keenly the importance of not relinquishing too readily the biological family with its traditional kinship networks. The family, she says, can be viewed as a phenomenon having an immutable foundation in biology, so, whatever view is taken, it must be realized that an individual's genetic profile is never a discrete programme of information relating to that individual alone. Parents' idiosyncrasies, when manifested in their offspring, she maintains, contribute a sense of "kinship identity" which it would be foolish to disregard. Almond also recognises this phenomenon, referring to it as, "a psychic similarity...a common Weltanschauung".

In her chapter, Strathern draws upon some anthropological studies conducted with a variety of family groups, which, whilst very different in their systems, all suggest a note of caution about the new technologies and their impact on families - a caution, she suggests, that is also evident in the

Nuffield Report on Genetic Screening (1993).

Confidentiality and secrets

Several contributors address the issue of the unavailability of information concerning their progenitors for children conceived with the assistance of donated sperm or eggs, or both. Subjects interviewed in the anthropological studies cited in the Strathern chapter bear out these concerns and Cole notes that secrecy and deception will work against the interests of children created in this way. Almond places emphasis on the need for records of the genetic parents to be kept with care and on the accessibility of these; she notes that in Sweden, once children have reached the age of eighteen, they have a right to know the identity of, for example, the semen donor. Donors, aware of this state of affairs, will no doubt take very seriously the implications of their donation, she adds.

Neil Leighton in *The Family: whose construct is it anyway?* makes a clear point that genetic origin is of critical importance to an individual - for it is the beginning of their "personal narrative". He supports his argument by looking at "open" and "closed" adoptions. "Open" adoptions, where the child has equal knowledge of both biological and adoptive parents apparently work out more successfully than "closed" adoptions where only the adoptive parents will feature. Leighton arrives at a general conclusion that legislation around adoption demonstrates a greater appreciation of the need for persons to have knowledge of their genetic origins than that which operates around the new technologies. With this legislation, Leighton tells us, "the myth is to be secured, and the truth obscured".

Ideologies - choices and outcomes

Earlier in this introduction, the point was made that due to high rates of divorce and separation and a growing preference for go-it-alone parenthood for partnerless individuals, traditional understandings of families and their structures are no longer fixed and unchallenged. Whilst these new structures have been with us for too little time to judge their efficacy for children, and, in broader terms, for society, it is upon this uncertain ground that we must address the impact of the new technologies.

Decisions about procreation and family structures rest upon adults, guided for the most part, by nothing save the compass point of individual preferences. For this reason, it is probably true to say that children's needs may not, in many cases, be at the centre stage of adults' deliberations. This is a further problem looked at in some detail by Neil Leighton in his chapter. Leighton is of the view that, when making choices about parenthood in whatever setting - natural, assisted or adoptive - we should have a special concern with the "outcomes" - the children themselves. For this reason, he urges that we work only with models which can ensure the necessary conditions of love, support and opportunity in its broadest sense, so that children might become "best imaginable persons".

Drawing upon evidence from the statuary care sector and from therapeutic services, Leighton provides accounts of children and their experiences which should strike telling notes for prospective and actual parents, who need to decide how best to proceed, as well as for those in the position of formulating policy for others. For example, Leighton records, "Children have clear perceptions from an early age as *one who is chosen* or *one who is not wanted*.. children resent being judged as *persons who may be allocated*.. children feel devalued by compromise in caring".

Of particular note, in his assessment of structures for children's care, Leighton draws evidence from the statuary system where he finds that the model most likely to succeed, is the one which simulates a "family atmosphere".

As we anticipate the millennium, society appears to need to establish what elements of this "family atmosphere" it would be beneficial to sustain. Traditionally, one prerequisite has been for a child to be the product of a loving heterosexual relationship with the couple committed to permanence. Some still maintain, and with good reason, that this model has the potential for providing sustainable growth and support for *all* family members, whether the child comes about through assisted conception, or naturally. However, for a variety of reasons, including a lack of adult confidence in the likelihood of achieving fulfilment through sustained commitment to couple relationships, confidence has been undermined in the nuclear structure itself. Thus, whether through pragmatism or cynicism, other structures for procreation and care are now envisaged.

Perhaps it is sufficient to lend support here to the principal of placing the child at the centre of our deliberations rather more than, in this climate of individualism, is currently the case. Almond warns of problems created for children through adults exercising *their* preferences: she notes a growing anger amongst the young caused, for example, by the re-jigging of families.

In *Choosing the Family*, Sandra Marshall conducts a rather wider examination of the issue of "choice", particularly with regard to the new technologies. In her paper, she also does some conceptual mapping in relation to the language and ideas embodied in the debate. Generally speaking, Marshall welcomes biotechnology as an extension of the control which people increasingly exercise over their reproductive lives. For her, children need not be left out of the frame, for they have possibilities for choice too: they could, if they so wished, choose later to divorce their parents! Within the family arena, Marshall believes that sympathy and support should lie with those who have *no* choice, rather than those who do. For example, she would not direct resources towards those who have chosen to have children in less than propitious circumstances. But, she cautions, with the opportunities afforded through the new technologies, choice may not be everything, and her descriptive "Harrod's list" model of choosing demonstrates a cynicism which could well undermine the valuable notion of a child as a "gift".

Does parenting, done as a private activity, make too great a demand upon parents? Should parenting be more of a collective responsibility? As Marshall reminds us, there is already, within technological intervention, a collective responsibility for producing a child, but for Martin Thomasson, in Chapter 5, it is "collectivity" in childcare as in procreation, which can offer distinctive goods over and above the exclusivity of the biological one-to-one. Thomasson uses Marge Piercy's utopian community - where "technology is used reflectively and caringly to enhance the lives of its inhabitants" - as a vehicle for exploring what he perceives as the four key elements of family: responsibility, commitment, intimacy and belonging. As Piercy describes, all children would be produced ectogenically, each having three parents. Within this model, what Thomasson terms as the "negative, exclusionary" issue, common with traditional forms of parenting, would no longer be in evidence. For Thomasson sees current problems with families as to do with *systems*, not with individuals, because biological parenting on the old model needs considerable "good fortune" and "heroism" in order to succeed. But, through biotechnology, relief is at hand, Thomasson claims, as it offers the possibility for us to re-organise our personal, relational lives, in that the "networked" family, presented here, would offer new systems of support and security. These are just those kinds of systems, it might be said, which Strathern and Almond see as already existing through biological kin connections!

In his *Bound to Care: Family Bonds and Moral Necessities*, Neil Pickering looks at the idea of family as a *given* - as something lying beyond our changing technological and political world. As part of this exploration, he draws upon an idea, "intuited reality", as suggested by Brenda Almond in her article, *Human Bonds*. Pickering places this idea alongside his notion of reproductive technology as allowing a departure from the traditional view of there needing to be clear biological links between the members of a family. With this conceptual departure, Pickering supposes, our understanding of family must rest on something that is more in the nature of moral or ideological. For he has a concern that the biological "givens" will be viewed as *natural and good*, whilst technological interventions, for example, in-vitro fertilisation, would, on this basis, be judged as *unnatural* and *bad*. This is a bias, he feels, which is sometimes employed by those whose business it is to regulate policy (for example, The Human Fertility and Embryology Authority). In part, Pickering resolves the problem by recognising that technological interventions may, in reality, be linked to the good, in that they do, in fact, offer "different environments for purely biological events to take place", at the very least, they are interventions in pursuit of human good.

In relation to the form the family should take, Pickering cites Rousseau who believed that families should be constructed with a basis in utility for they need to provide a suitable vehicle for the care of the young who cannot take care of themselves. In this context, Pickering provides critiques of two models, offered (in this book) for the framing of future families as alternatives to traditional nuclear structures. These models, "the liberal", resting largely upon individual choice, and "the utopian", offer quite specific, new contexts for procreation and care. Generally speaking, Pickering is keen that critically important matters are assessed, as far as possible, in ways which lie "outside the norms of a particular ideology, culture, religion or society".

Couples and others

The contributors to the earlier chapters of this volume broadly concern themselves with families and social change and, in particular, with what opportunities and challenges there are around the new reproductive technologies. Whilst the final papers touch on some of the themes brought in earlier, the concern in the last section of the book is not so much with family groups concerning *children*, as with *adult* relationships. In some ways the issues of choice and control and of ideologies in relation to personal and procreational needs are dealt with in these papers too, but the prime concern here is to present a critique of traditional couple structures, especially marriage.

In *Justifying Monogamy*, Steve Wilkinson challenges the belief that attitudes towards sexual relationships have changed in any real sense, for he says that we still live in a "couple culture" in which monogamy is seen as "desirable and good". This arises, Wilkinson believes, from normative claims about what sex *ought* to mean. In a carefully argued paper, Wilkinson investigates the principles underlying this monogamous culture as he sets out arguments to undermine its justification.

For Bob Brecher, in Chapter 10, the couple culture, as expressed through marriage, is a working demonstration of a political and social ideology, for marriage, he asserts, is "ideology at work". He notes with regret that, latterly the homosexual community has also been enticed by the "haven in a heartless world" image of the permanent couple state. But, he asserts, exclusive intimacy is not a good intimacy, for marriage can restrict, even prohibit, that altruistic cooperation on a broader scale which should be sought in our society. Brecher is critical of this "private act with its public meaning" and draws on Lévi-Strauss when he typifies marriage as "the archetype of exchange".

For Paul Gregory, in the final chapter, it is in the very fact that marriage is no longer of *economic* necessity for individuals that the source of its weakening may be traced. He notes in couple relationships, a shift from the practical and the material, to the personal and the emotional and this, he believes places unnecessary burdens on individuals. If "well-rounded persons" fail to fit into "the square holes of marriage", then it is the fault of a system (of values), not of individuals, Gregory argues. However, he believes that this particular state of affairs (where couples who are parents cannot survive together) is not necessarily detrimental for the care and upbringing of children, and he offers, in his chapter, some different kinds of domestic structures which might represent "home". In his conclusion, Gregory muses on why it is that the bringing up of children should dictate how adults should live (with regard to the practical and relational structures they should sustain), for at least half of adult life is *not* taken up with children. By implication, these writers are arguing for more atomised, individual existences outside traditional family structures.

Perhaps this is already happening. In *Justifying Monogamy*, Wilkinson quotes the Archbishop of Canterbury, who says that "gratification and emotional fulfilment" are nowadays "divorced and decoupled from lifelong commitment". Some may judge this as one outcome of the current primacy, in personal relationships, of an individual's "right to choose".

Concluding remarks

It may be the case that technology expresses what science should be about - the extension of human happiness through choice. Advances which today may shock and appear beyond the pale of human acceptance may, in a few years' time, be commonplace. Notwithstanding, all innovation is liable to harbour values which may not be welcome to future generations so these must be unpacked and judgements made of their efficacy, or otherwise. The question which must be asked, therefore, is not, "Is it old?" "Is it new?" but - "Is it right?"

In the past twenty years or so these reproductive technologies have, in biological terms, challenged our perceptions of procreation and the family. Where one marriage in three ends in divorce, and one child in three is born out of wedlock, our perceptions are likewise challenged as we witness a whole variety of preferences and ideologies at work within the family arena. Unfortunately, for society, it is likely to be a generation before the outcomes of these experiments may be judged. In real terms the so-called "Liberal" or "Utopian" models are as yet unproven for children as against the traditional nuclear pattern of two parents nurturing their own biological offspring. Perhaps, for the sake of future families, we could use the biotechnology debate as an opportunity to focus our attention on what happens *after* birth, rather than *before* it.

1 Family relationships and reproductive technology

Brenda Almond

According to Caesar, in ancient times Gaul was divided into three parts. It appears, today, that the same may be true of parenthood, which has suffered three tripartite divisions. The first is the triple division of fatherhood - biological, legal and social; the second the tripartite notion of motherhood, as genetic, gestatory (or birthing) and commissioning. The third is a triple notion of parenthood itself: biological parenthood, legal parenthood, and the holding of parental responsibility.

At the same time, it seems there may be a developing social consensus, led by utilitarian philosophers as well as some feminist theorists, and encouraged by certain lawyers and health economists, that technology has brought us into a new age of relationships by choice, and that this is something to be unproblematically welcomed. The latter is however, a remarkable assumption in view of the history of family bonds in the story of the human race. It may well seem equally remarkable to anyone who has had direct experience of parenting and, in particular, of giving birth, and who takes time to reflect on these experiences. These are purely contingent considerations, of course, but it must at the outset be conceded that philosophy alone is unable to provide a challenge to such claims, and that any challenge must involve at least some reference to the kind of facts that social anthropology and related disciplines can provide, as well as, perhaps, to some introspective reflection on one's own experience as child, parent, spouse or other kin relation.

It is clear, however, that very different assumptions have guided human thinking on these matters in the past. Some indication of this is to be found in literature, legend and folk-lore. In particular, there are those stories and traditions which centre on what might be called the Cinderella experience. In the familiar version, the not-biologically-related child is used and abused by step-parent and step-siblings alike. Similar stories abound of wicked stepmothers - or fathers - as well as the more intangible but ubiquitous myth of the changeling. It is worth asking, what is the point of this myth? What *is* a changeling? The answer must be that it is someone who lives in an intimate situation with those who are, biologically-speaking, strangers or, from the other point of view, a stranger who invades a situation of close intimacy. Without any knowledge of the science of genetics, those who framed these stories had in mind a scarcely tangible web of connections and expectations - a sense or expectation that the absence of the biological link would mean an absence of what might be called psychic similarity: shared attitudes, appraisals, interests, tendencies, common qualities of character, a common *Weltanschauung* - a characteristic way of looking at the world. Of course, we all know that none of these things can be assumed, even where relationships are indisputable, but total breakdown or absence of common sympathies is regarded as extraordinary, and provides the stuff of tragedy and disillusion.

It is interesting to contrast the position I have described - that relationships are and should be a matter of choice - with that put forward by Hegel in *The Philosophy of Right*:

> In substance marriage is a unity, though only a unity of inwardness or disposition; in outward existence, however, the unity is sundered in two parties. It is only in the children that the unity itself exists externally, objectively, and explicitly as a unity, because the parents love the children as their love, as the embodiment of their own substance . . . a process which runs away into the infinite series of generations, each producing the next and presupposing the one before. (Hegel, 1952, p.117)

The contrast between natural and artificial, biological and social, is starkly presented in these two different approaches. One explanation for the emphasis on the social, is that some relationships are indeed socially generated - that is to say, relationships by marriage. But even at the level of popular culture, there is recognition of the existence of relationships which are not merely social alongside those which are, and the responses these evoke are commonly quite different in quality. One may compare, for example, popular attitudes to mothers with those to mothers-in-law. Many societies, then, including both primitive cultures and complex modern ones, distinguish socially-created relationships from blood-relationships, seeing the latter as special and immutable. This double-sidedness is well described by Marilyn Strathern, an anthropologist with a particular interest in kinship networks:

"Family life," Strathern writes, "is held to be based on two separable but overlapping principles. On the one hand lies the social character of particular arrangements. Household composition, the extensiveness of kin networks, the conventions of marriage - these are socially variable. On the other lie the natural facts of life. Birth and procreation, the inheritance of genetic material, the developmental stages through which a child progresses - these are naturally immutable." (Strathern, 1992, p.17)

One might add - although this is part of what is at issue here - that, even the changes made possible by new technologies, cannot negate the essential *naturalness* of conception, pregnancy and childbirth, the relationships they create and those on which they depend. So why should some people think otherwise? Why deny what to many people will seem obvious - the deep importance of human kin connections?

A possible answer to this question is provided by the British legal theorist, John Eekelaar, who argues that to a very large extent, parenthood is a social and not a natural concept. "All attributions of parenthood are social" he writes, "so the choice is not between "social engineering" and "following nature", but between different kinds of "social engineering"." (Eekelaar, 1993, p.81) Eekelaar's views rest on a double foundation. The first is a particular view of the role of law; the second, a commonly held assumption about the role of society in relation to the duty of care of the young. It will be most useful to consider these two aspects separately, before going on to consider some of the more specific issues involved here.

The role of law

Eekelaar sees law as active, not a passive by-product of social change - as leading, not following, social convention. In this he follows the legal historian Roscoe Pound in rejecting the Hegelian thesis - later developed into a new and more general theory of law, ideology and society by Karl Marx - that law is a reflection of social progress and development (Pound, 1923, pp. 151-2). From the point of view of moral philosophy, this theory could be said to run parallel to the emotive theory of ethics, which, in a similar way, portrays *moral* language as dynamic rather than descriptive, as seeking to influence others rather than to inform them - as attempting to evoke action and alter attitudes. The term used by Pound to describe this dynamic or active function of law was "social engineering" - a term which, as Eekelaar points out, is often used pejoratively today, although Karl Popper, in *The Poverty of Historicism*, used it with favourable overtones (Popper, 1945).

15

Popper's sympathetic perception, however, was based on a conception of social engineering as small-scale and limited in scope, and he chose it in order to paint a contrast between the humdrum and unambitious goals of the engineer - a kind of social repairman - and the Utopian architectural blue-prints of totalitarianism. I suspect Popper would see attempts to change the natural structure and basis of the family by means of a pincer attack from medicine and law as having more in common with the latter than the former.

Eekelaar supports his general perception that law does in fact lead rather than follow in these areas by appeal to the legal ruling that a husband is presumed to be the father of a child, when it is born to a woman living in a marital relationship with him. *(Pater ist quem nuptiae demonstrant.)* He speculates as to the reasons for this, in part interpreting historical attitudes by appeal to recent developments - for example, new legislation concerning surrogacy, and the recent refusal by a judge to allow DNA "finger-printing" for purposes of establishing paternity. (It should not be overlooked, however, that it has become a well-established procedure in cases involving immigration applications.) He concludes that these recent judgements, like the rules that have prevailed in the past, are to be understood as expressing the primacy of social over biological parenthood. Their implication is, he says, that parenthood is indeed socially engineered.

This is to overlook, however, an important, indeed crucial, point as far as an appeal to past practice is concerned - that the capacity to establish parenthood reliably through DNA fingerprinting is an entirely *new* development which was quite simply not available to earlier generations. Previously unconceived-of possibilities now exist - take, for example, the remarkable capability of establishing the identities of bodies thought to be those of the Russian Tsar and his family by comparing their DNA to that of known descendants of the family. Indeed, in view of such possibilities, it could well be argued that both the recent legislation in the United Kingdom (e.g., Section 30 of the Human Fertilisation and Embryology Act 1990) and the decision of the judge in the case cited, are actually ill-conceived. Whatever view one takes of the new legislation, however, it would be foolish to overlook the fact that the older approach to confirming paternity would of necessity have been based on pragmatic rather than theoretic considerations. In earlier times, conclusively establishing paternity would have been, in most circumstances, an impossible task - except, of course, in those cases that the law indeed recognised, where the husband was physically apart from his wife for the relevant period. For clearly, under normal circumstances, the only way for a woman to be sure of the fatherhood of her baby would have been to have intercourse with only one man during her menstrual cycle. The law - or any outsider - would be obliged to assume that she *might* have had intercourse during this period with her husband, so there could be no *better* founded claim than his, even if there was evidence of a concurrent adulterous liaison. But to suggest that what must be legally presumed is the whole of the story would be to deny commonsense, which even in the past was prepared to cast a glance, whether jaundiced or ribald, at striking physical resemblances of children to persons outside the family circle. A legal convenience does not, then, require one to interpret the facts in such a way as to see the case of human procreation as totally distinct from reproduction in livestock or plants - a rose is a rose, not the alien stock on which it is grafted.

So while it is no doubt right to say that law is not invariably to be seen as merely following, or describing social convention, there are limits to its scope for creativity - for moulding the relationships between people by *fiat*. Indeed, it is often the other way round. As Marilyn Strathern points out, the very notion of a parent in Western thought evokes the idea of a social relationship. Moreover, such a conception of kinship has implicit within it an expectation of a closeness of understanding and empathy, a "crisscrossing network of similarities" of character (to lift a metaphor of Wittgenstein's out of context), and an expectation of service and sacrifice which is, more often than not, actually forthcoming. It is these natural tendencies and inclinations, on the whole, that have provided the signposts which have supplied a direction for law to follow over its long evolution.

This is to place a considerable weight on kin relationships, but it is hardly surprising that humans should attach importance to these - particularly the parent-child relationship - when other species defend their young to the death and when, as has been claimed, even the organically simple tadpole is able to recognise differentially siblings, half-siblings and unrelated individuals. But evidence from the animal kingdom is not essential to this case. The Greeks, whose literature and philosophy have exercised so much influence over modern thought, saw blood relationships, particularly those between parents and child, brother and sister, as absolute and as morally exigent. It is interesting to note that the Oedipus story would lose its point, its sting, if *social* relations were regarded as primary - the whole point of that story is that social relationships were being impeccably played out amongst people whose biological relationship made this wholly inappropriate. To kill a father - even one you have never met before - was an inexpiable crime, as it was to violate a mother, even one who had never known or nursed her child.

Eekelaar, however, in a kind of modern updating of these Oedipal possibilities conceives of a case in which biological, legal and responsible (or caring) fatherhood are separated. He is concerned about a case, *re O*, in which biological fatherhood was preferred over social parenthood.(1 FLR 77). In his own hypothetical case, the biological father, A, is an anonymous

17

sperm-donor playing no further role; the legal father, B, is the man with whom the mother was living at the time of the birth, but from whom she has separated, and the responsible father, C, is the mother's new husband who has been granted parental responsibility. For Eekelaar, the significant person in this situation is C. Parental right and responsibilities should go to him for: "Parental responsibility should always be associated with the exercise of social parenthood." (Eekelaar, 1993). He argues, therefore, that the United Kingdom's Children Act (1989) is wrong in its underlying presumption that biological parents have responsibility for their children, and in its attempt to attach social and legal responsibility to biological parenthood.

Eekelaar's view, in contrast, amounts to an assertion that biological parenthood is in itself negligible. But if this is what is being claimed, it has wide implications. To begin with, it involves endorsing a common but simplistic view of artificial insemination by a donor as a simple *medical* procedure. And secondly, it involves seeing as unproblematic developments in *in vitro* fertilisation which have led to the detachment of motherhood, too, from its biological meaning. Initially, the transfer of an egg from a willing donor to a woman desperately wanting to bear and raise a child may seem to raise few ethical difficulties, but technological possibilities do not stay tidily within the bounds of this relatively uncontroversial scenario. Instead, they open up a "slippery slope" of devastating potential. Examples are not hard to find: the possibility of harvesting viable eggs from a fetus means that an aborted fetus could now be a genetic mother; eggs taken from women in their twenties have been successfully implanted and brought to term by women in their late fifties; while developments in intensive care have made possible the gestation and delivery of a baby to a dead woman whose womb and reproductive system have been kept artificially functioning. To regard any of these developments as of purely medical significance would be a mistake. Their social implications are dramatic, and their possible psychological and emotional effects as yet unknown. At a minimum, one might say that to be born under some of these circumstances would indeed be to be an orphan in a sense previously unknown to human beings. It would be to be born already an exile from the kinship network.

These considerations suggest, then, that one should pause and look very carefully at what might be called the "hard-headed" assumption that gametes are detachable, that genetic relations are negligible. Initially, this is to rely on an intuitive response, a sense of ethical affront - perhaps, even, as Mary Warnock described it, a feeling of "outrage" (Warnock, 1987). This reference to feeling is best understood in relation to her earlier defence of the role of moral sentiment in an article called *The artificial family* (Lockwood, 1985). But it is not hard to find practical arguments to lend weight to these reactions. To begin with, the consent of the donors, particularly of the young women who donated their eggs, may well have been secured on quite different tacit assumptions about the destiny of those eggs. In view of the breadth of possibilities, therefore, there is a case for interpreting "informed consent" quite strictly in this area.

But secondly, the "hard-headed" approach may be based on some unrecognised factual assumptions about the quality of care that can be relied on where purely social connections are involved. Indeed, I would suggest that there is a need for a new judgement of Solomon here. In the biblical tale, Solomon recognised that the true - i.e., the biological - mother, would prefer even to sacrifice her own rights and her relationship with the child if that was necessary to preserve the child's life, and that it was *for this very reason* that her rights and relationship should be preserved. I would suggest that things are not intrinsically different today, if one considers, for example, recent abuse cases connected with children's homes to which children have been taken, often on the grounds that this is necessary to protect them from possible abuse by their natural parents. Who can be trusted with children? Clearly parents cannot always be, and children must sometimes be removed from their care, but it is far from self-evident that other carers are less fallible.

Role of society - the duty to care

But for Eekelaar, the problem is compounded by the fact that he does not attribute to the parent even a direct duty to care. Instead, he sees the responsibility for looking after children as falling on the state, or society in general. Everyone, he says, has a general obligation to "promote human flourishing", and a specific obligation derived from that to care for the newborn . He concedes, however, that society may best fulfil this obligation by imposing a duty of care on biological parents. Thus, a natural duty is neatly inverted in Eekelaar's argument, to become a derivative, social or indeed legal duty, rather than a primary, ethical one. The immediate consequence of this is that society might well fulfil its duties in a number of different ways, any of which would be equally morally acceptable. These would include various kinds of social parenting.

For comment on this, we must once again turn to social anthropology. Eekelaar seems to be overly influenced by the fact that different societies may deal with the problem of child-care in different ways. For example, Eekelaar would probably find useful support in the fact that in some tribes a woman's brother is responsible for a child, not its natural father. Nevertheless, while variation in social arrangements is possible, and while, of course, there have even been societies ignorant of the connection between sexual intercourse and child-bearing, the idea of a blood-tie has on the whole been the idea of something immutable and non-negotiable. As I have commented elsewhere: "A person's "sisters, cousins and aunts" - narrow-minded uncles, bad-tempered brothers or handicapped son or daughter - are part of the baggage of life." (Almond, 1988)

Nor is it only the parent-child relationship that is involved. For where there are "real", i.e., blood relationships, these have wider implications - something that Eekelaar's discussion, which remains narrowly focussed on parents and children, completely ignores. These connections are not isolated facts and their social relevance spreads out in a widening circle. Strathern writes: "In many cultures of the world, a child is thought to embody the relationship between its parents and the relationships its parents have with other kin." She adds, "Until now, it has been part of most of the indigenous cultural repertoires in Europe to see the domain of kinship, and what is called its biological base in procreation, as an area of relationships that provided a given baseline to human existence" and "It is an extraordinarily impoverished view of culture to imagine that how we conceive of parents and children only affects parents and children." (Strathern, 1992, pp. 31-34 *passim*)

This was so widely taken for granted until recently that it came as a surprising discovery to our legislators a few years ago that grandparents had no status in British law. And yet, with the ubiquitous breakdown of marriages and *de facto* partnerships, it is to be expected that contingent relationships could assume greater rather than lesser importance.

It is worth noticing, too, that social work practice and local authority provision in the past - together with "community care" today - work on quite the opposite assumptions from those implied by the "social construction" view. While certain philosophers promote the view that advanced reproductive medical techniques are to be welcomed as expanding *choice* - making it possible for any kind of relationship to be created or abandoned at will - social workers are routinely required to seek "real" relatives and attempt to convince them of their moral and social obligation to change the whole pattern of their lives to accommodate sick, senile or disabled kin. And, of course, descent and lineage continue to be regarded as of crucial legal importance as long as inheritance is considered a just way of passing on wealth.

Eekelaar, in contrast, seems to see the primary family relation as confined within the duality of parent and child. He does, however, recognise that certain moral and legal concepts have a part to play in this relationship. Whilst rejecting any conception of rights as independent entities and describing them as "intellectual constructs", he nevertheless recognises a complex of rights and reciprocal obligations involved in the parent-child relationship. In particular, he argues that children have rights, in the sense of what they "when fully informed and mature, would be likely to have chosen." (Eekelaar, 1993) He distinguishes recognition of these rights from welfarism, which he defines as basing arrangements on some external judgement as to what is in the child's best interest.

I will not discuss this account of rights in detail, since the central issues here do not depend on agreement about their analysis. Most would agree, however, that morality cannot be based entirely on rights without appeal to other moral concepts. It is true, too, that it is not necessary to invoke children's rights in order to talk about parental duties. And thirdly, Eekelaar is undoubtedly correct to point out that the attribution of a right is not to be confused with another person's judgement of where someone's interests lie. One can undoubtedly have a right to what is *not* in one's interest, and not a benefit - it is not for the football pools promoter, for example, to judge whether a prize-winner's life is likely to be ruined by his sudden access of wealth before deciding whether to award the prize. Nor is the question of what *is* in fact a benefit the same as the question of whether it is what someone *wants*. But of course it is true that one will only *claim* what one, at least in some sense, wants. (Though some people are perverse enough to claim or want something *only* because they conceive of it as their right and not because they have some independent reason for desiring it.)

Applying this to the case of a child in relation to a parent, these considerations would imply even more strongly that there is a residual notion of a right not covered by the child's interest, benefit or even choice. If this is so, then it would be wrong to base judicial decisions concerning a child's care simply on the child's best interest as judged by a third party. To do this is, in any case, to ignore the question of *parental* rights. Rather than being, as many believe, qualified and provisional, these are important and substantial rights, grounded in parents' duty to care for their children. This conception of parental rights can be derived from the Kantian principle that "ought" implies "can." In other words, society would be inconsistent to declare that there is a parental duty to care without conceding a parental right to do so. If this is conceded, it follows that parents have a direct moral obligation to care for their children. If society does not permit them to care for their children, it prevents them from fulfilling that duty and thus violates their rights.

Other arguments may, too, be advanced for the priority of parental rights. Not without weight is the quasi-biological argument derived from Hobbes that there is at least some attenuated concept of ownership of children that is analogous to people's ownership of their own body. Recognition of this claim can only be intuitive, for it can hardly be grounded on any extraneous considerations. Nevertheless, the biological argument need not stand alone. For it may be ranged alongside an argument of a political nature relating to the conditions necessary for cultural and religious freedom. Conceding parental rights, it can be argued, is the best and most effective way to limit the power of the state over the individual. Totalitarian projects, both philosophical and actual, have tended to encroach upon and limit parental control and family influence, while even under liberal regimes, where benign motives may be presumed, there is a continuing danger of the state usurping private prerogatives.

Ferdinand Schoeman has added a moral argument to this essentially political one: that the right of parents to exercise power over their children is based on their own justifiable moral claim to a certain kind of intimate relationship. He writes: "Why should the family be given extensive responsibilities for the development of children? Why should the biological parent be thought entitled to be in charge of a family? I believe that the notion of intimacy supplies the basis for these presumptions." (Schoeman, 1980, p.14) Schoeman's argument, then, is that close human relationships require as their setting privacy and autonomy, and that a parent's right to this type of private relationship overrides even some limited cost to the child.

It has to be admitted, however, that some situations make a choice unavoidable. In these situations, in which there is a conflict between adults' and children's wishes, there is growing willingness to involve older children themselves in the decision. Eekelaar suggests that the question of who *initiates* social care may be settled differently from decisions about later arrangements, when he proposes that the child's own wishes should play a part.

There are, however, difficulties with both halves of this strategy. First, where an early choice by others is concerned, what of the wish a child might retrospectively have for its own (genetic) mother or father? The "constructivist" view seems to involve permitting early decisions which would in effect deprive the child of this, which may indeed later come to be seen by the child as the only and important option. As for the idea of allowing a child later in life the possibility of choosing a new social family - something that has recently happened in the USA - it is unlikely that this could provide a stable base that lasts for life, generating responsibilities as well as benefits. What, one wonders, might become of the traditional network of expectations of kin support later in life, particularly where there are adverse changes in circumstances? Would the "chooser" child, when adult, accept a member of his or her "socially chosen" family for expensive or self-sacrificing care? Would the socially chosen family, conversely, accept a child "chooser" back to their care if adult life brings that child disability or hardship?

The inclination to answer "no" to these questions is based on a perfectly sound and rational conception of the notion of choice. A "chooser" on the whole, wants only what is pleasant and rewarding - that is the whole point of choice. But life, on the other hand, is a mosaic of darker and lighter patterns. And "chooser" children are unlikely to volunteer for what is not personally satisfying. Indeed, there is a chance that such children would be unwilling to care for their elders even through social and community measures, whether taxes or charitable contributions. Nor is the loss entirely on one side. For children, too, there is the loss involved in losing the possibility of a relationship for whom their whole "narrative" is familiar - those irreplaceable persons who have known them "all their lives", in the familiar phrase.

But these are perhaps highly abstract reflections, and it might be difficult to see what they might imply in practice. In conclusion, then, it will be useful to return to some of these practical recommendations.

Right to be informed of biological parenthood

In Sweden a child born by AID has a right (at 18) to know the identity of the semen donor, but the latter has no rights of legal paternity. In Britain, officially recognised agencies accepting sperm from donors must record their identities, but, as things currently stand, this is to be kept confidential, even from the child. In contrast, practices in France in this matter are very different. Donation is strictly limited to two or three occasions; donors are married men with children, and their offer to be sperm donors is discussed carefully with both the men and their families (Novaes, 1994).

If the considerations that have been advanced in this chapter have any weight, then it would seem that such donors should recognise that they are indeed fathering *children*, and that children should be guaranteed access to information about them. This said, it has, of course, to be recognised that the procedures involved are simple and in the end impossible to regularise or police. People might, however, be less willing to assist with "irregular" donation if aware that this might have legal implications.

The issue of fatherhood, however, may seem straightforward when compared with the new complexities involved in the notion of motherhood. Sections 27 and 28 of the 1990 British Act referred to earlier define a mother as the "carrier" of a child, whether or not that child is genetically hers. However, under Section 30, a woman who carries (gestates) a child but hands it over to a couple as a result of a surrogacy agreement, ceases to be the legal mother, just as in the case of adoption. This ambiguity is hard to resolve practically. As far as intuitive judgement between the claims of a genetic and a gestatory mother are concerned, there is much force in Raimond Gaita's view that it is inconceivable that a child conceived *in vitro* would have the same interest in seeking out his natural parent as one conceived in the ordinary way (Gaita, 1991, p.42). I think, however, that the genetic connection might continue to exert some fascination, or at least curiosity, were someone aware of an origin of this sort. This unavoidable conflict, however, should alert us to the unprecedented severing of links that may be a consequence of such procedures. The least that is required here of the law is that it should not lend its weight to the suppression of information about biological parenthood and in particular, that it should ensure that, as far as possible, records are maintained and are accessible to those desiring information - possibly without direct identification - of their origins.

Whose responsibility is it to care for children?

In general, most people would probably agree that parental responsibility should be associated with the exercise of social parenthood. This means that it should in many cases be extended to long-term cohabitees and step-parents. But there may be tension here between the early claims of the mother and the long term claims of the father. Indeed, there are some grounds for saying that modern European and North American societies are moving towards matriarchy as a result of insensitive taxation policies which make little or no allowance for family responsibilities, and social provision unintentionally destructive of family life - for the more provision is made for single parents, the less need there is for partnership between the sexes. A single mother in a recent interview remarked "If it weren't for the help I get from my mother and grandmother, I don't know what I'd do." - a remark that was revealing, in that it pointed to a demographic shift in the source of reliable support. It uncovers a situation that research might well show to be far more common than is generally acknowledged, and the social consequences of which are wider than the immediate family unit.

Conclusions

Variations in the traditional family are not unique to modern times. In particular, step-parents and step-siblings are no new phenomenon, although the reasons for their existence have changed. In the past women's high mortality, particularly in relation to childbirth, was the cause of remarriages and new relationships, while today the cause is more commonly a matter of the breakdown of relationships, divorce and remarriage. It is worth noticing in relation to this observation that, for children, parental mortality would almost certainly have been a more acceptable reason for their own step-status than adults' choices, since these can be seen as a betrayal. It is not surprising, then, if, in some cases, today's restructured families generate hostility. This hostility may well be responsible for a variety of social ills, including homelessness amongst teenagers who have run away from unacceptable or intolerable domestic circumstances, and abuse, particularly sexual abuse by an unrelated adult living in close domestic proximity to a sexually pubescent child.

In *Fertility and the Family*, Jonathan Glover recommends "letting the future shape of the family evolve experimentally" - taking "control of our own reproductive processes." (Glover, 1989) But this is, I would suggest, a dangerous doctrine. Family bonds are the cement of social existence and are not subject to construction and destruction by something as fragile and volatile as individual choice.

The process of fractionalisation, then, that has led to the threefold division of parenthood is dangerous, and the conclusion to be drawn from this is, I believe, that no steps in the area of reproductive medicine should be endorsed by legal change or social acceptance until some body of limited experience has been built up as a guide to the overall social implications. In these matters, in other words, it is foolish to rush in where even angels are justified in displaying a cautious conservatism.

Note

The author wishes to thank Derek Morgan and Gillian Douglas, the editors of *Constituting Families: a study in governments*, (Franz Steiner Verlag, Stuttgart, 1994) for permission to use her contribution to that volume: "Parenthood: fact of nature or social construct?" as the basis for the present chapter.

Bibliography

Almond, B. (1988) "Human Bonds" *Journal of Applied Philosophy*, 5, pp. 3-16

Eekelaar, J. (1993), "Parenthood, Social Engineering and Rights" in Morgan, E. and Douglas, G. (eds.), *Constituting Families: a study in governments*, Franz Steiner Verlag, Stuttgart.

Gaita, R. (1991), 'Parental rights and responsibilities' *Quadrant*, Sept. 1991.

Glover, J. et. al. (1989), *Fertility and the Family*, Fourth Estate, London.

Hegel, G. W. F. (1952), *The Philosophy of Right*, trans. T. M. Knox, Clarendon Press, Oxford.

Hobbes, T. (1981), *Leviathan*, Macpherson, C. B. (ed.), Penguin, Harmondsworth. First published 1651.

Lockwood, M. (ed.) (1985), *Moral Dilemmas and Modern Medicine*, Oxford University Press, Oxford.

Novaes, S. (1994), *Les Passeurs de gametes*, Presses Universitaires, Nancy.

Popper, K. (1961), *The Poverty of Historicism*, 2nd edn., Routledge & Kegan Paul, London.

Pound, R. (1923), *Interpretations of Legal History*, Cambridge University Press, Cambridge.

Schoeman, F. (1980), "Rights of children, rights of parents, and the moral basis of the family", *Ethics*, 91, pp. 6-19.

Strathern, M. 1992), *Reproducing the Future: anthropology, kinship and the new reproductive technologies*, Manchester University Press, Manchester.

Warnock, M. (1987) "Do Human Cells have Rights?" *Bioethics*, 1987, 1. pp. 1 -14.

Warnock, M. (1985) "The Artificial Family" in Lockwood, M. (ed.) *Moral Dilemmas and Modern Medicine*, Oxford University Press, Oxford.

2 New families for old?

Marilyn Strathern

The family in the 1990s . . . is one of the pieces of armoury with which political and philosophical debate is conducted.

(Morgan and Douglas, 1994, p. 10)

In commenting on arguments for and against change in the context of legislative measures to deal with commercial surrogacy, Sybil Wolfram[1] offered the following ethnographic insight. She presents it by way of background material for a readership otherwise unfamiliar with British parliamentary practice.

> Background on political argumentation and English law is necessary to disentangle the dispute about surrogacy in England. In political settings, arguments are often voiced not because they are necessarily believed but because they are effective in achieving or preventing a piece of legislation. These may be termed "political arguments". English historical evidence shows that arguments of a certain *content* are peculiarly persuasive and occur on one side or the other whatever the particular subject under discussion, whether it is the divorce laws, laws about incest, allowing prohibited relatives to marry, or surrogacy. We can call these "political *platforms*." The most common arguments, or platforms, in favour of a legislative change in England are that it is not really a change, or is a consequence of a change already made; that it opens to the poor what is open to the rich, or to women what is open to men; and that it brings England into line with Scotland (the two countries were unified only in 1707 and still have different private law). Conversely, effective arguments against change are that it is a change, will cause other changes,

27

discriminates against the poor or women, or widens differences between England and Scotland. (1989, pp. 189-90 notes omitted)

The family in the age of biotechnology finds itself the subject of similar argumentative practices; the way in which the family itself is construed in English culture[2] also provides insight into how such platforms get made.

Arguments

Political arguments are, as Wolfram glosses them, distinguished from others "by the fact that the object of voicing the arguments in question is not just, for example, to pass the time of day or clear one's head or advance learning but to effect or prevent a particular practical change" (Wolfram 1989: p.196). She adds that there will also be arguments about specific social consequences to be expected from the practical change in question. But while social consequences seem important to the collective body, Wolfram observes that they tend to be indecisive because good and bad outcomes are usually evenly matched. As we shall see, however, thinking about whether outcomes are likely to be good or bad can draw on the same argumentative content that she identified as a potential political platform, namely whether or not a change is *really* a change. Debates over biotechnology, at least as its development affects human reproduction, frequently turn on claiming either that there is nothing new in the new reproductive technologies or else to the contrary that there is everything that is new.

This particular platform is by no means confined to debates in parliament. If public discussion about the new reproductive technologies takes a similar form then it is for one crucial reason. These technologies can be considered as instruments of change themselves, indeed as already having caused change in the way people think about the reproductive process. Everyone is faced with "new" things to think about, and thus with how their own opinions may be altering.[3] Here is everyman speaking (a Berkshire Post Office worker):

> Do people feel all these changes are for the good and are we ready for them? Medicine is racing well ahead; do we morally feel we are in agreement with what they're doing? We probably need time to catch up with the medical people where things will change over the years. *I suppose, given enough time, we will all start to think differently.* (quoted in Hirsch, 1993, pp. 91-2, original emphasis)

Is thinking differently, like the technologies themselves, to be welcomed or feared? Will people really think differently? Whether or not the changes are

28

"real" may well contribute to people's sense of continuity with the past or else of forward-looking innovation in the way they make up their minds.

The same questions apply to the family (O'Donovan 1994, p.42). What is interesting about English ideas of the family, when they run alongside ideas about technological or social change, is that advocacy for and against change can draw on pre-existing suppositions about stability and instability in family forms. They can be approached from many perspectives[4]; here I choose two. How these two perspectives afford argumentative platforms for thinking about whether biotechnology brings real changes will become apparent.

Perspectives on the family

I refer to pre-existing suppositions in order to underline the cultural place that the family has long held in the way the English consider it to act as a register of both change and continuity (cf. Strathern 1992a). The kinds of relationships family members sustain among themselves may be interpreted in either direction, and concomitantly as either responsive to or in resistance to society at large. All this constitutes the first perspective.

The first perspective takes change and continuity from the viewpoint of "society" and takes the family as a set of social relationships. Consider the following common images. On the one hand, the family is seen as perpetually in crisis, a fragile bonding of persons who do not bond as well as they should, the victim of rising divorce rates, of drop-out children and of increasing bureaucratic meddling/neglect. On the other hand, the family stands for the continuity of generations over time, for the place where intimacy and support are guaranteed by habit, for the knitting together of self-interest and moral concern far stronger than any transient legislation or adolescent fad, and with an immutable foundation in biology. The significant contrast is that in the first view family form reflects changing social conditions from the outside as well as from within, whereas in the second it endures despite them. The particular negative and positive values can of course be reversed.[5] The family that struggles with adversity may also be drawing creatively on its own internal resources, even as changing social circumstances allow experimentation with new family forms (e.g. Weston, 1991). Instability is not always negative: resourcefulness and enterprise can make the family a creative element in society. Stability may not be what it seems either, if what endures are old oppressions. Indeed the continuity of family forms, as in the conventional "nuclear family", may be taken as endorsing social values some would prefer to discard (Cole, this volume).

The permutations are endless; the point to note is the *diversity* of arrangements that characterizes the family as a cultural institution. All these features belong to the way the English can present "the family". The family thus offers a ready-made domain for debate about what is old and what is new, both in family life and in society at large. Indeed the family may be seen as much a part of society as set apart from it.

In this first perspective, then, change and continuity as taken from the viewpoint of "society", the family may be understood either as a part that belongs to and is responsive to the whole or else as separate from the rest of society and affording an independent commentary upon it. As a result, it is possible to think of change as affecting the whole (society as evinced in its constitutive elements - change all of a piece) or as affecting a part (change taking place in some areas will not necessarily affect changes in others).

The second perspective repeats this possibility. This is the perspective from what one might call "nature", although, since this entity cannot articulate for itself such a perspective, it is necessarily constituted in the relationship people *perceive* between nature and society. The perspective brings into focus the extent to which the social forms of family life deal with given and immutable facts of human existence. Here social intervention stands for the potential of change itself. The "social" element of human life thus becomes a point which may be taken either as a part of the whole (the conditions of human existence) or as set apart from it (what is given and immutable).

The perspective from nature is in the present context the perspective from "biology" and the capacity of social arrangements to deal with biological facts. What is at issue for the family is its basis in kinship. Kinship rests in ties which in the twentieth century English hold are created twice over. They are created through the process of reproduction, involving sexual partnership, birth and infant nurture, and they are created again in the social forms of human life built up after these conditions of existence (above all, marriage, and the family as a household or living unit). This distinction between the biological and social elements of kinship, one that has now passed into general parlance (cf. Strathern, 1992b), gives rise to diverse permutations as to what is to count as kinship.[6] Kinship is apparent as an amalgam of these elements, a hybrid construction.

Biotechnology concerns the family as a reproductive unit. While it is perfectly possible to procreate outside a "family" context (even in an "anti-family" one), for the most part, procreation is thought to bring together persons *as* a family. If family members are regarded as bound to one another through the act of procreation, how they thus come to be related is held to have consequences for how they *do* relate - get on, interact - as social persons. This relationship between the natural "facts of life" and the family as a social unit has its bearing on how the past is read and the future imagined. Here biotechnology slips into arguments about what is old and what is new, more or less as Wolfram predicted. And, as she noted, the question whether or not a change is a real change can occur on one side or the other, and this is as true of people wondering whether to fear or welcome these innovations as of those whose task it is to implement change. The caution or enthusiasm people voice may be reflecting their own sense of how opinions and values do or do not *really* change.

The amalgam of biological and social facts, joined but distinct in the English view of kinship, allows change to be seen either in the part or in the whole. The second perspective offers the same argumentative platform as the first. If one alters one element does it or does it not have consequences for the other element?

Arguments for and against change

Arguments in favour of embracing the new reproductive technologies can point to them as techniques that will alleviate suffering and provide remedies for disability, and thus enable the family to take its proper and traditional form. The domains of biological and social fact are not, in this view, to be confused. Medical intervention is strictly intervention in the biological process. And while it may alter the disposition of kin, that is, alter expectations about who becomes related, the traditional family as a social unit is not necessarily challenged (cf. Dolgin, 1990). If the form it takes is that of two parents and their children, then the form is preserved regardless of how the parents are created. Indeed, reproductive medicine can overcome disabilities which stand in the way of the full flowering of family life: technology thus appears to be attending to biomedical problems already in existence. As a consequence, we arrive at the following powerful formula: the techniques may be new but the problems are old.

There is an analogy between the supposition that new biomedical techniques such as *in vitro* fertilisation assist old biomedical problems (infertility), and the supposition that new social arrangements (involving anonymous gamete donors, say) can assist old ones (traditional family life). Provided the distinction between biological and social issues is sustained, the analogy can be rendered as a chiasmus (at least in respect of two of the terms). It is possible to argue that the new biotechnology does not necessarily create new *social* issues: supporting change in one area (medical assistance to overcome biological defect) without introducing a change that might be disruptive in another (deleterious to the family as a social institution). Change is only in the part, not the whole.

Arguments against technological change, on the other hand, may be based precisely on the grounds that one change *will* lead to other changes and that change in a part implies change in the whole, including new life for old iniquities. Much feminist commentary, for instance, has pointed to the "new"

31

social power that the dispensers of technology accrue under a regime of "old" patriarchy.

From another direction, the facilitations of gamete donation and embryo transfer, not to speak of gestational surrogacy, may be seen to "disturb" the very biological basis on which family relationships are founded - as Mary Warnock (1985) implied in pointing to entirely new possibilities for contested motherhood. Wolfram (1987, p. 210) notes that the moral objection to surrogate motherhood being raised by Warnock in the mid-80s is a further consequence of fusing ideas about motherhood with ideas from a quite different domain, notably the domain of commerce. Her message is that cultural domains are not insulated from one another. This is an evident case of one social possibility (becoming a mother for third party) leading to another (wishing to become pregnant for money). What about biological possibilities?

Insofar as the biological component of procreation was that very part generally acknowledged as autonomous or natural, that is, free from human intervention, intervening at all may be regarded as changing "nature". Arguments that the new technologies lead to unnatural outcomes fall into this camp. At the same time, intervening may be regarded as inherent to "human nature" in its form as human enterprise. Such creativity may be assumed to be unstoppable, a common view of scientific advance; what it gives rise to are the kinds of questions about limits on which Warnock was so eloquent. How does one indeed impose limits on human enterprise?

Those in favour of change may well separate the problems from the techniques (the problems are old, the techniques new), yet so sometimes do those who are more cautious. On the other hand, those against change see new problems accompanying new techniques, or old problems being given new life, but either way inseparable from the power that the techniques bring, yet this last is also a platform upon which enthusiasts for innovation may stand. Techniques for argument, at least, seem endless.

Evidence

I have suggested that the family fuels certain perceptions of change and continuity, not least when its own constitution in kinship points to an internal dynamic. The amalgam of biological and social relations creates a hybrid of elements at once distinct and joined. It thus seems as possible to change one without changing the other as it seems impossible not to change one without changing the other. These contradictory possibilities can arise either from separating the parts or from imagining an inseparable whole. Arguments concerning the 'relationship' between Technology and Society[7] often follow a similar pattern. By way of evidence (of these kinds of argumentative platforms) I refer briefly to positions in respect of developments in gene therapy and genetic screening before returning to the biological and social relations of kinship. These come from two reports, one an enquiry by a non-statutory body (the Committee on the Ethics of Gene Therapy) required to report to Parliament, the other the report of a Working Party established by an independent body (the Nuffield Council on Bioethics) prepared for public information. Both are concerned with what kinds of changes should be feared or welcomed.

Caution and enthusiasm: the reports

In the first, technology is seen as a potential tool in the service of society. The 1992 Clothier Report on the *Ethics of Gene Therapy* opens with the words:

> Every significant development in science or technology has been accompanied by dangers both known and unknown. Society watches this progress with mingled admiration and anxiety . . . to prohibit the progress of science in any particular direction may well be tyranny; to seek to shape its course is surely sensible. In doing so we should be careful also to preserve *the right of society* to determine how the achievements of science are used. (Clothier, 1992, Foreword, my emphasis)

The usefulness of the tool also requires the reassurance that it is a solution to problems rather than a harbinger of them. It seems rational to support the advent of new techniques if it is the techniques alone that are new, and the case seems particularly strong when they address old problems in the context of well-established (old) social practices. The Clothier Report focuses on one particular set, namely the practice of ethics committees in medical research. The Report recommended that somatic cell gene therapy should be regarded in the first instance as research involving human subjects. More than "medical practice" is involved (attending to the individual patient); defining such therapy as "research" would involve a certain kind of critical scrutiny (for scientific merit, the legal implications and wider public concern). But the point is that guidelines for such critical review are already in place. As research, gene therapy could and should conform with these already existing guidelines ("accepted ethical codes"). The Committee was thus able to support the case for the development of somatic cell therapy[8], and hence investigation in this area, that is, the case for technological change, by arguing there was no change in the accompanying ethical issues. While

33

therapy is, in the conclusion of the Report, "a new kind of treatment . . . it does not represent a major departure from established medical practice, nor does it, in our view, pose new ethical challenges' (1992, p. 25). Change in technology does not, in this formula, necessarily mean change in society. These are parts of modern life that work to this extent independently of each other.

By contrast, the 1993 Nuffield Report on *Genetic Screening: Ethical Issues* opens not with a division between technology and society but with their fusion or convergence, so to speak, in a statement about knowledge:

> New knowledge about human genetics, and the links between genetic inheritance and susceptibility to disease, have important ethical implications . . . what uses might be made of this knowledge? Who should share it? What are the implications for people identified as having an abnormal gene or genes? For their families? For society? (Nuffield 1993, p. 1).

Its focus is thus on the effects of knowledge. I believe it moves towards the view that society does not so much have to establish a right to use already existing achievements, as Clothier wrote, as recognise that it already determines the conditions under which knowledge is produced and disseminated. Society and technology change together. The Nuffield Report also goes out of its way to bring into focus a social object: genetics, it observes, "inescapably involves families" (ibid., p. 4). As a consequence, the Report argues, it is the very status of genetic information as such which "raises ethical questions that differ significantly from the normal rules and standards applied to the handling of personal medical records" (ibid., p. 3).[9] Information about the genetic endowment of any individual person is inevitably information about those closely related to him or her. At the same time, genetic knowledge has developed to a point where it makes sense to screen for disorders which may affect a population but may or may not affect the individual being screened. In neither case is the individual an isolated medical subject.

What is at issue here, then, is unprecedented as far as medical information is concerned. The Report certainly does not advocate abandoning genetic screening - on the contrary, it flags its enormous potential - but it does recommend that such screening should be accompanied by monitoring and counselling services to keep possible repercussions in check. It talks of possible adverse consequences, and points explicitly to the danger that old iniquities might be increased; for example, ethnic groups might find themselves "additionally stigmatised" by their genetic profiles (ibid., p. 77). This is an argument for enthusiasm insofar as the medical potentials of genetic screening are concerned, and for caution insofar as technological change cannot only be technological. Technology and society in this sense form a whole.

Varieties of caution: the families

If debates about what is new and old can draw on some of the family's enduring ("old") characteristics, namely its reputation as at once stable and unstable and as evincing both change and continuity in its social forms, then English families in the late twentieth century have in turn, through exactly the kinds of debates on technology and society to which I have been referring, *new* fuel for their self-definitions. Evidence of a kind comes from two cases examined during the course of an enquiry conducted in 1990-1 into, more or less, what people think that living in the age of biotechnology might mean as far as procreation is concerned (Edwards et al, 1993). To a remarkable extent, the people in this study felt that they should clearly endorse or clearly criticize the changes they saw afoot. In providing their opinions on the matter, however, they tended to strike a general note of caution.

The evidence comes not from those who have themselves had experience of reproductive medicine, although everyone had heard one way or another about test-tube babies and surrogacy. Rather the purpose of the exercise was to learn what kind of sense people make of some of the possibilities offered by reproductive medicine when they are not directly involved. It was in the first instance an exploration into how an anthropologist might set about gathering such information: the "people" were women and men with whom sustained conversations were held in situations where other information already existed on their social and cultural backgrounds.

I draw briefly from Jeanette Edwards' conversations in Alltown in the north-west of England and from Eric Hirsch's interviews with couples living in London and the south-east. In both cases the anthropologists were returning to people whom they knew, Edwards to a small town where she had carried out ethnographic research, which meant that she was able to put the men and women with whom she talked into a social context; Hirsch to couples, scattered in location, for whom the common context was primarily a cultural one, namely their previous interest in having participated in research on information and communication technology in the home. "The family" had entered into the previous studies to somewhat different effect. One of the ways in which Alltown residents described themselves was through classifying certain families who live in the town, whether born and bred in Alltown or "incomers", while Hirsch's study had focused on the use to which families as households put technology. Taken together, this previous work presented versions of the dual images of English family life noted earlier. On the one hand, families are regarded as congeries of relatives with an ancestry, and thus attached to places, newly come to any one particular place or not. On the other hand, families also expect to form households, functional units concerned with the process of day to day living and thus responsive in their behaviour to conditions outside. These dimensions, it is important to note, are present in both cases. However, Alltown residents were in a position to relate certain sets of kin to town history and its present divisions, whereas the south-eastern couples were being questioned about how they made the household work.

To its residents, Alltown seems internally divided. The idea of there being certain "close knit families" offers images of social inclusion and exclusion (Edwards, in prep.). A number of well known families represent this effect of family in general. They are said to intermarry, and both to fight among themselves and to respond in unison to outside threat ("kick one and they all limp"). Some are simply "big" families; others may be identified by "real" or "proper" Alltown names.

Family in this sense is already a link with the past, even as certain key kinspersons are said to be. The presence of families indicates the roots (*their* idiom) that individuals have with the past; the inevitability of such roots in turn poses one of the problems Alltown people perceived in reproductive medicine (Edwards 1993, pp. 60-2). The perception does not have to depend on the respondents themselves belonging to long-rooted families; it is enough that "family" indicates "belonging", so that even if a particular family is not rooted in one place its individual members are rooted *in it*.

The problem was voiced during the course of a discussion at a creative writing class. Edwards stimulated a conversation that led one woman to observe that it was all very well talking about "scientific things", but such possibilities also led one to think about other family arrangements. The discussion had touched on anonymous gamete donation. The woman, herself a mother with four children, wanted to draw a parallel with adoption and cited the case of an uncle of hers who had been adopted. "I don't know how much he wondered about his real mother but his adopted mother was always his mother from his point of view" (quoted in Edwards, 1993, p. 61). From this perspective, the consequences of gamete donation would be no different ("I had a discussion with me mother some time ago and something to the effect that it wasn't blood necessarily that counted, it was the relationship that you'd built up"). But then she mused on the implications of people trying to find out their origins, brought on by the discussion of "scientific things": "but that can always be disturbed by, as you [Edwards] say, adopted people growing up and wondering and trying to find out where they actually came from: which I can imagine will also take place with those who want to find out what laboratory . . . because they felt they somehow belong somewhere".

36

And: they will "want to know which box they slot into" added another member of the class.

Adoption and step-relations cropped up several times in the conversations, as parallels for the way one might think about the relational consequences of surrogacy arrangements or gamete donation. Indeed the parallels served as vehicles for thinking about the relative weight one would give to particular connections or about the awkwardness that might have to be managed on a day to day basis. In this sense, we might recall the Clothier Report. There too the committee decided on a parallel, namely between the development of gene therapy and medical research, and they determined that what was relevant on the day to day basis of practical ethics were existing guidelines for ethical practice concerning research on human beings. Alltown people were also drawing, as it were, on existing guidelines. They were rooting these new possibilities via expertise they already had at their fingertips, namely their expertise as kin, so that their own past and present experiences provided guidelines for dealing with and thinking about the way relationships worked out between persons. It was with a measure of confidence that some, at least, took the discussions in their stride.

Kinship expertise showed in talk about dangers in the "power" of "scientists". God and Hitler were both invoked (op. cit., pp. 62-3). For people were explicit not only about psychological problems (the trauma in store for individuals, given that "truth will out") or biological ones ("interbreeding" in ignorance of origins), but about the consequences for kin relationships. Technological intervention, as Edwards summarizes their arguments, could disrupt existing relationships or create novel but antagonistic ones. She writes: "The dangers posed to existing relationships are rendered visible in ideas put forward about ambivalent kinship roles, conflicting claims on children and "interference" in relationships which ought to be enduring" (op. cit., p. 63).

These are arguments for caution. The very separation of problem and technique (society and technology) facilitates this caution. For rather than solving old problems (though they are acknowledged also to do that) or drawing on old social practices (as the Clothier committee referred to accepted ethical practices), in these views the new technologies are seen to *lead to* enduring problems in social relations making their reappearance.

The Alltown arguments stress the continuity of certain fundamental facts of family life, and the inevitability of these facts leading to future problems arising from technological intervention. It is not just that "truth will out", but that a person's attachments are formative, including bodily attachment before or after birth, as are idiosyncratic habits of parents and kin that contribute to the person's own individuality, so that it *matters* which persons a child grows up with. The new interference suggested by reproductive medicine - one that does not arise in the case of step-parenting or adoption - was the thought of babies "brought into the world by scientists" without, in the words of one woman, "any real beginnings or real ancestors or family" (op. cit., p. 59). [10] These concerns were set side by side the acknowledged heartache of childless couples; the issue was not whether "scientists" pressing forward with these innovations (whether they should or not) but rather about the continuity of kinship facts (what was to be done with them). Having to manage relationships would endure as long as kinship endured, and this was a problem for families. The technologies might be new but these problems were old ones; Alltown people spoke with the authority of their practised knowledge.

In many respects the people with whom Hirsch talked responded in similar ways and drew on a similar battery of concepts. Hitler was invoked in connection with the dangers of controlled reproduction, adoption was offered by way of a parallel and people voiced fears about "standardising" persons. Nonetheless Hirsch's conversations took him in a different direction.

A primary concern lay in the consequences that follows from new possibilities of exercising choice. Like Edwards, Hirsch (1993, pp. 68-9) comments on the diversity of opinion he heard. These fall into roughly three sets according to his classification, each of which makes a connection between the exercise of individual choices and the totalitarian implications of such choice being in the hands of society. [11] Thus some stressed the unbridled consumerism implied in "baby shopping", others entertained a futuristic vision of a Brave New World, while between these extremes lay the accommodations that couples offered in working out their own existing relationships. More so than in the Alltown conversations, people were imagining new worlds for themselves. Change enters into these arguments, but in a somewhat different way. The assumption already there is that one lives in a changing world, apocalyptic or no, to which every small change will add its effect. Technology and society change together: what we do now is already bringing the future into being. And technology may well contribute to the making of new problems, as was voiced in the observation from Hirsch, (pp. 91-2) quoted earlier. One woman, a pharmacist, said in connection with the idea that men and women might be able to 'decide' what kind of child they wanted: "It's difficult to say what the point (of control/limit) is though, isn't it?" Because what would be sound now, in ten year's time, the improvements in science and the improvements in technology, who's to say the barriers won't move?" (quoted in Hirsch, 1993, p. 91).

If one were to differentiate these responses from those of the Alltown residents, it might be in terms of the couples' emphasis on the ramifications of what is new, and in some cases their reflection that what they are thinking now is going to contribute to how things will be in the future. In the Alltown case, persons were located within families and in places with roots, and this presumption of continuity sat side by side with perceived continuities in kinship problems. What kind of locations were being imagined by these south-easterners?

Hirsch's conversations elicited a view of family life as a *project*.[12] I am perhaps over-influenced here by an original case study (see Hirsch, 1992, p. 213ff) which he chose to describe for its exemplification of an extreme form of domestic consumption.[13] But it is arguable that this family has systematized values more generally held. They sustained a busy and highly organized existence, their home connected internally through an intercom network with family members conscious of needing to be at once liberating and systematic about the pursuit of "activity". The children were openly encouraged to be active - so purchasing a video carried the risk of increasing the passive watching of television where purchasing a video camera would encourage the children to make things for themselves (ibid., p. 218). Behind this lay not simply the nurturance of individuality: it is desirable that children grow up to be active rather than to be passive. At the same time, the family provides an important environment for co-operation and social skills. So when a spectrum computer led to quarrelling, the solution was to find a non-competitive form of software programme. If the family's interests are conceptualized as over and above the demands of individual members, then, it is because the family too is seen as a functioning concern. The model which family members have of themselves and the world they create through their enterprise would seem to feed into what they see themselves as creating in the future: they are prepared for novelty, and they nurture persons to have a hand in their own destiny.

Here technology and society form a potential whole. These are exactly the grounds on which advocates for change might imagine whole new worlds: the possibility of new family forms eliminating many old problems. The enthusiast would want to bring biotechnology and social engineering together. Martin Thomasson's account of Piercy's radical feminist utopia offers an example [this volume]. Hirsch, however, encountered *utopia* being evoked to strike a note of caution - the dark side of the Brave New World. If the note of caution echoes that of Alltown, the reasons are rather different. They lay, I surmise, in people's focus on the power of their own creativity.

When people, who live in a family that is itself a future-oriented project, think about living in the age of biotechnology (also projected into the future) then one problem that comes to the fore is the management of desire and aspiration. Desire and aspiration are what lead one into the future one hopes for. But these cannot be unlimited. As someone else, talking about genetic engineering and the choices available to intending parents, observed:

It was something that came up when we had our discussions [about tele-shopping] previously that . . . people would rather sit at home . . . in front of the television, than go out and shop. But I don't believe that, and I don't think that will ever happen because people will want to go out and shop because the desire to be with other people is much stronger than using a computer to save them energy. So I think in the same way that, something has been developed, research and so on and it may be possible . . . to create this perfect being, but I think pressure from society, from people, will say all right you've created that, but we don't actually want that, that's not what we're looking for. (Hirsch, 1993, p. 70, emphasis removed)

Without straining the comparison too far, I would point to echoes here with the way the Nuffield Report considers the relationship between technology and society. Enterprise has everyone at the ready to seize new opportunities. The question is thus how to constrain desire: do we really want what some might think we want? So the Report recommends constraint, for example, on the aspirations of insurance companies who might otherwise seize this opportunity to gain information about the health and condition of clients in order to enhance the companies' competitiveness. [14]

These are problems that may have "old" antecedents. But they are "new" in a crucial sense that arises from the imagined fusion of technology and society. [15] The technological implementation of an individual's aspirations and desires will be implementations that belong to particular times, places and societies, and thus carry values others do not necessarily have, and which the future may not welcome at all. What makes human creativity as problematic as it is hopeful, in this view, may well be the possibility of its realisation.

In sum, there are no "new" or "old" families here. But discourses that seek out what is new and old can always find evidence of a seemingly concrete kind in family life. Families can be presented as much in terms of ancestral connections and their rootedness in the past as in terms of their functioning as enterprising and creative units in producing for the future. These past and future orientations themselves offer views on the future and the past. The first orientation (the rooted family) projects into the future long-standing concerns to do with the relatedness of person with which any technological innovation must deal; the second (the enterprising family) recalls from the past the kind of greed and totalitarian impulses that have accompanied human enterprise throughout history.

Acknowledgement

I am grateful to Brenda Almond for her invitation, and to Ilana Ben-Amos for assistance with preparing the manuscript. The stimulus of Jeanette Edward's and Eric Hirsch's work will be evident.

Notes

1. I cite Wolfram not only as one of the few anthropologists who has published recently on English kinship (*In-laws and Outlaws* has the subtitle *Kinship and Marriage in England* (1987) but because she was as much a philosopher as an anthropologist. A version of this chapter was presented to St. Hilda's College, Oxford in June 1994 as a memorial lecture to her.

2. Much of Wolfram's data concerns legislation, and she is careful to distinguish the law in England from the law in Scotland. As far as the surrogacy case is concerned, she notes that legislation seems neither to include nor to exclude Scotland, and she refers to both England and Scotland as, "loosely", "England" (1989, p. 190). Her usage suits the cultural gloss I would give "English", as a variety of Euro-American discourse.

3. Newness does not necessarily imply change, whereas it would be hard to speak of old things without implying some kind of continuity with the past. The terms do not work quite in parallel even though the one is often taken as the measure of the other. Campbell (1992) separates the *new* as in the sense of fresh or regenerated ("new shoots", "new year") from the innovative which is an improvement that may be part of a long line of developments (a "new type of battery" or "new, improved" product), and from the novel or unfamiliar ("nouvelle cuisine"). However he points out that different neophiliacs may determine the newness of things in different ways, and what may be novel to one person may be simply innovative to another.

4. See for instance those of contingency and choice raised by Sandra Marshall (this volume), or Chadwick's dimensions of individualism and communitarianism ("The family provides a focus for dispute between (these) rival political philosophies" (1994, p. 62)).

5. In English culture, or Euro-American culture at large, either change or continuity can be valued or de-valued. Stability may be given a high value when it is associated with tradition or the natural order and a low value when it is a sign of stagnation or the heavy hand of the past, even as instability may

be welcomed for the creative spaces it opens up and feared for its disruptiveness. Enlightenment can be attributed alike to the past (an unalienated society) or the future (a liberated one), as may oppression (stultification or anarchy). Change and continuity thus invoke expectations of some kind of past and some kind of future, and the issue for argument is generally at what point on what continuum between past and future do present practices fall.

6. These permutations afforded by the cultural distinction (between biological and social facts) work to merographic effect (Strathern, 1992a, pp. 72ff), as I have tried to demonstrate in moving between the two perspectives ("from nature" and "from society").

7. Whereas "society" is often an encompassing term (it would include "technology") for anthropologists, this is not the case in general parlance where "social" issues are often set off from others.

8. This was stated in the specific context of pursuing the development of somatic cell gene therapy. I do not want to distort the Report's own messages of caution. Germ line gene therapy was separated off as problematic for the future; the Report also notes that while gene therapy "will be a new resource in medical practice and will raise the familiar ethical questions attending any novel form of treatment . . . it may also introduce new and possibly far-reaching ethical issues which have not previously had to be considered" (Clothier, 1992, p. 2). These include taking decisions on behalf of the unborn. Two years on, Warnock is quoted as saying of *germ line* therapy that parents are always making decisions on behalf of their children and deciding to have germ-line therapy would be just another similar decision (*New Scientist*, 14 May 1994).

9. What is of concern here is the private status of *information* about genetic conditions; the Clothier Committee was faced with a different situation (the purpose of gene therapy is to alleviate disease in the individual patient). I should add that the Clothier Report noted that local research ethics committees are in support of a national body for the review of research practices in this field; in endorsing this, the Report adds that it regards continuing supervision of gene therapy as necessary.

10. She went on to say: "Somebody somewhere must be creating this artificial womb. A baby reacts to what you're feeling - if your heartbeat is faster then the baby's heartbeat is faster. It could be fed on just vegetables - how would it react then, through the placenta - not what you fancy like

crisps, or salad, or Chewitts on the bus, like cravings at different times - vegetables, sweets alcohol whatever it takes to make a baby. It will have no feelings because no feelings are going through it." (Edwards, 1993, p. 59)

11. A version of the dispute identified by Morgan and Douglas (1994, p. 8) as between "individualism and collectivism (communitarianism)" in family law.

12. A characteristic marked in styles of family life described by Schneider and Smith (1973) some years ago in their study of middle class families in Chicago, and alive and well today in the aftermath of Britain's Enterprise Culture (Hirsch's study was carried out in its heyday).

13. The family has five children of whom two are adopted; the father describes himself as a technologist or inventor.

14. Citing a futuristic view from 1935 of the kind of knowledge that might be available to insurance companies, the Report comments that, "it is only in the past few years that molecular technologies have provided *the opportunity to realise (this) goal"* (Nuffield, 1993, p. 65, my emphasis).

15. A father of four children observed: "And you really can't differentiate between biological experimentation like that and filling the world with nuclear arms, because it's the very same thing, science is following research as far as it will go." (Hirsch, 1993, p. 80)

Bibliography

Campbell, C (1992), "The desire for the new: its nature and social locations as presented in theories of fashion and modern consumerism", in R. Silverstone and E. Hirsch (eds.), *Consuming Technologies*, Routledge, London.

Chadwick, R (1994), "Moral reasoning in family law: a response to Katherine O'Donovan", in D. Morgan and G. Douglas (eds.), *Constituting Families: A Study in Governance*, Steiner, Stuttgart.

Clothier, C. (1992) *Report of the Committee on the Ethics of Gene Therapy*, H.M.S.O. London.

Dolgin, J. (1990), "Status and contract in surrogate motherhood: an illumination of the surrogacy debate", *Buffalo Law Review*, 38: 515-550.

Edwards, J. et al (1993), *Technologies of Procreation: Kinship in the Age of Assisted Conception*, Manchester University Press, Manchester.

Edwards, J. (1993), "Explicit connections: ethnographic enquiry in north-west England", in J. Edwards, et. al. in *Technologies of Procreation: Kinship in the Age of Assisted Conception*, Manchester University Press, Manchester.

--- (in preparation) "Gametes need names: relatednesss and relationship in late twentieth century England" [manuscript, University of Manchester].

Hirsch, E. (1992), "The long term and the short term of domestic consumption: an ethnographic case study", in R. Silverstone and E. Hirsch (eds), *Consuming Technologies: media and information in domestic spaces*, Routledge, London.

Hirsch, E. (1993), "Negotiated limits: interviews in south-east England", in J. Edwards, et. al. in *Technologies of Procreation: Kinship in the Age of Assisted Conception*, Manchester University Press, Manchester.

Morgan, D. and G. Douglas (eds.) (1994), *Constituting Families: a study in governance*, Steiner, Stuttgart.

Nuffield Council on Bioethics (1993), *Genetic Screening: Ethical Issues*, London

O'Donovan, K. (1994), "Love's law: moral reasoning in the family", in D.Morgan and G. Douglas (eds.), *Constituting Families: a study in governance*, Steiner, Stuttgart.

Schneider, D. M. and Smith, R.T. (1973), *Class Differences and Sex Roles in American Kinship and Family Structure*, Prentice-Hall, Englewood-Cliffs.

Strathern, M. (1992a), *After Nature: English Kinship in the Late Twentieth Century*, Cambridge University Press, Cambridge.

Strathern, M. (1992b), "The meaning of assisted kinship", in M. Stacey (ed.) *Changing Human Reproduction: Social Science Perspectives*. Sage, London.

Warnock, M. (1985), *A Question of Life: the Warnock Report on Human Fertilisation and Embryology*, Basil Blackwell, Oxford.

Weston, K. (1991), *Families We Choose: Lesbian, Gays, Kinship*, Columbia University Press New York.

Wolfram, S. (1987), *In-laws and Outlaws: Kinship and Marriage in England*, Croom Helm, London.

Wolfram, S. (1989), "Surrogacy in the United Kingdom", in L. M. Whiteford and M. L. Poland (eds.), *New Approaches to Human Reproduction: Social and Ethical Dimensions.*, Westview Press, London.

3 Biotechnology and the 'moral' family

Phillip Cole

Section 1. The "moral" family

Developments in biotechnology in the area of human fertility are usually portrayed as a reproductive "revolution" that challenges the "traditional" family. Depending on your viewpoint, it is either a welcome ally in the struggle against the oppressive patriarchal-based nuclear family; or it is a danger to the moral fabric of the community. My purpose in this essay is to argue that the reality is quite opposite to this portrayal - the practice of biotechnology in reproduction has been to reinforce a particular "moral" structure of the family, and those who criticise the traditional family cannot look to biotechnology for any aid in challenging it.

By the "traditional" family here I mean: two heterosexual adults, one male, one female, in a formalised relationship of marriage, parenting a number of children to whom they are biologically related. That relation is that the couple produced the children through sexual intercourse with each other, and the woman gave birth to the children. An additional but important element of this traditional model is that each parent has clearly defined roles: the adult male procures resources for consumption within the family by working outside it; and the adult female works within the family to nurture and sustain it.

There are two dimensions to the traditional model: the natural dimension and the social dimension. By the natural dimension I mean the biological relationships between parents and children - the genetic connection. By the social dimension I mean the socially constructed roles and relationships within the family: the roles of "parent", "father", "mother", "son", "daughter", "child", and the relationships between them; these are all, to some extent, social constructs. The role of "parent" within the traditional family, for

47

example, goes far beyond merely having a specific biological connection with children. These two dimensions of the family can, of course, come apart: we can have the social family without necessarily having a natural family with the usual genetic connections, as families constructed through adoption show.

The structure of the family has been the focus for political debate, with support for the traditional model coming from both the "old" and the "new" Right. Certainly, the political leadership in Britain has claimed that this particular model has a central role to play in maintaining the social and moral fabric of society. Some have blamed the rise in crime over the past 30 years on the decline of the traditional family model and the rise in numbers of single-parent families. At the centre of the controversy is the claim that families need fathers: the absence of father-figures in families leads, in the long term, to delinquency amongst children. The claim seems to be that the father-figure is a "moral presence" needed for the proper moral education of children.

The traditional family is, therefore, the "moral" family, and is an essential component of the good society. Anything that threatens to disrupt the "moral" family is therefore a threat to the community as a whole - and if the reproduction revolution threatens to disrupt family structures, then it threatens to disrupt society itself, and must be controlled. It is inevitable, therefore, that there should be a legal framework in place to control biotechnology as it affects the family. My concern in this essay is with that part of the legal framework that aims to control who shall and who shall not be permitted to be a parent. The reproduction revolution widens the scope of parenting decisions, both in the sense of allowing a wider range of people to decide whether to be parents; and in the sense that it gives the state and its institutions greater scope to control who shall and shall not be parents. The framework of control and constraint, I will argue, has as its primary goal, not the welfare of children produced through reproductive techniques, but the maintenance and protection of the "moral" family, and the subsequent maintenance and protection of the traditional "father-figure" role within it.

Section 2. The legal framework

(a) Fatherless families

There are three levels of control over the application of biotechnology - (i) the law; (ii) the guidelines issued by the Human Fertilisation and Embryology Authority; (iii) the guidelines devised and followed by the fertility clinics themselves. In this section I will look at the legal framework.

One aspect of the reproduction revolution that clearly challenges traditional family structures is that women can become pregnant without having to come into direct contact with men. Donor Insemination (DI) means that single women and women in lesbian relationships can gain access to sperm through fertility clinics, such that the biological father is now an anonymous sperm donor who has no further role to play. Biotechnology therefore increases scope for the growth of fatherless families.

However, those who framed the 1990 Human Fertilisation and Embryology Act clearly saw this as undesirable. The Act (Section 13 (5)) says:

> A woman shall not be provided with treatment services unless account has been taken of the welfare of the child who may be born as a result of the treatment (including the need of that child for a father) (Morgan and Lee, 1991.)

"Treatment" here refers to any medical, surgical or obstetric services provided for the purposes of assisting women to carry children (Section 2 (1)) (Ibid.). While these provisions do not rule out supplying DI services to single or lesbian women, they certainly make it clear that fatherless families are not to be encouraged: there was, in fact, enormous pressure in Parliament to restrict fertility treatment in law to married couples only.

Margaret Brazier comments:

> The tenor of the Act as it emerged from Parliament is to attempt to limit assisted conception to couples living in a traditional family structure. (Brazier, 1992, pp.287-8)

And she says:

> ... whenever arguments are advanced to ban AI for women without a male partner, those arguments should be analysed carefully. Is the essence of the argument that *any* woman without a male partner should not be helped, or that lesbians should not be allowed to use AI to have children? I suspect it is often the latter. (ibid., p. 265)

Derek Morgan and Robert Lee comment that the law "has all the hallmarks of a profamilist ideology" (op.cit., 1991, p. 146). They say:

> Assisted conception is to be, for the most part, for the married, mortgaged middle classes; a conclusion which is entirely consonant with infertility services being unavailable on any scale through the NHS. (ibid., p. 146)

The Act's demand that the clinics should consider the "welfare" of the child amounts to consideration of the fitness to parent of applicants for treatment. In other words, it is a screening system for parents, similar to that used in adoption. To the response that this is a proper concern, Morgan and Lee reply:

> That we do indeed exercise an increasingly sophisticated and pervasive continuing licensing system of the fitness to continue parenting does not mean that we are thereby justified in extending that regime back before birth or into pregnancy. (ibid., 1991, p. 147)

The reality, of course, is that people who apply to fertility clinics are not being judged on their record as *parents*, as they most likely have not been parents before: they are therefore being judged as *potential parents*. In the case of single women or lesbian applicants, a judgement has been made that women as such, lesbian or heterosexual, cannot meet the welfare needs of their potential children to a sufficient level to merit treatment. And the implication of this is that single or lesbian women who *do* have children are, because they are women, failing to meet the welfare needs of their actual children. The problem here is that the argument is dependent on a very ill-defined concept of welfare, without offering any clear criteria of what would count as a sufficient capability to meet the welfare needs of children.

(b) Families with fathers

It was argued in Section 1 that the traditional family has both a social and a biological structure. In the case of Donor Insemination (DI) or In Vitro Fertilisation (IVF) where sperm and/or eggs are donated, the social and biological structures of the family come apart. The legal response has been to set aside the natural structure of parent/child relations altogether, to preserve the traditional social structure of the "moral" family. In the case of DI this was first established by the Family Law Reform Act 1987, which ruled that where a married woman received DI with her husband's consent, the child is, in law, the child of the woman and her husband. The Human Fertilisation and Embryology Act (Section 27 (1)) says:

> The woman who is carrying or has carried the child as a result of the placing in her of an embryo or of sperm and eggs, and no other woman, is to be treated as the mother of the child. (ibid.)

The child has no legal claims against its biological parents, and they have no rights or duties against the child. And so a child produced through IVF with donated sperm and eggs could have four parents: a social mother and social father; and a natural mother and natural father. However, the law preserves the traditional two-parent family by abolishing the natural parent-child relationships and establishing the social parent-child relationships. The social structure of the "moral" family is therefore preserved. Of course, this could be interpreted as a progressive step, in that biological connections are being over-turned in favour of social ones; but the purpose of the law here is, in the end, reactionary, in that the aim is to rule out new forms of the family, and to protect at least the surface appearance of the traditional model.

(c) Confidentiality

One area of controversy in DI, and IVF treatment where it involves a donation, is the extent to which the children produced through these processes have a right to know their origins. A comparison is drawn with adoption practice. Adoption services advise that children should be told, at the earliest opportunity that they are adopted. The British Agencies for Adoption and Fostering advises prospective adopters:

> You can't keep adoption a secret because children have the *right* to know about their past and not to be kept in the dark. And, after all, there's always the danger that someone else will tell the child without any warning. Finding out like this can be a terrible shock to a child. So it's important to be honest and to discuss adoption quite naturally, right from the start. (British Agencies for Adoption and Fostering, 1986, p.16)

It is also believed that adopted children have the right, not only to know about their status, but also to know about their origins: that knowing who their natural parents are is essential to their identity formation - depriving them of such information is felt to be potentially harmful to their welfare. Under Section 26 of the Childrens Act 1975, adopted children therefore have the right of access to their original birth certificate at 18 in England and Wales, 17 in Scotland. Children of donation have no such corresponding right to know their origins, although they do have the right to basic genetic information about the donors under Section 31 of the 1990 Human Fertilisation and Embryology Act. However, the medical profession advises secrecy in such cases, so that the children of donation would have no knowledge of either their origins or their status.

Dr Alexine McWhinnie has argued that this inconsistency is an injustice. There is an analogy between adopted children and children of donation:

> ... since the children in both cases are reared by parents other than both

their genetic parents and because there is an artificially created situation where the adults in a child's world have information about the child that they can decide to share or withhold. (McWhinnie, 1986, p.17)

However, others have urged caution about extending Section 26 of the Childrens Act to cover children of donation. Katherine O'Donovan argues that the concept of identity being appealed to here needs to be subjected to critical scrutiny. This concept "is produced by legal and social structures which attach value to concepts of identity linked to genitors" (O'Donovan, 1990, p.102). She says:

> The hidden agenda of Section 26 is that adopted children have an unrequited desire to know their genitors, and that this is a natural and understandable need which can be met with legislation.
> Before we leap into extending Section 26 of the Childrens Act 1975 to cover all children with "unknown genes" perhaps we should investigate further the research data on adopted children. (ibid., p. 103)

The initial flood of applications under Section 26, says O'Donovan, has diminished to a trickle.

However, even if we accept that the sense of identity that rests on the need to know biological origins is a social construct which the majority of adopted children have successfully overcome since 1975, serious problems remain for the children of donation. Most would agree upon the importance of adopted children knowing their status as early as possible, if not their specific biological origins. Children of donation do not even have access to this information, and are therefore in a situation in which their parents possess power over them in terms of secrets that could have an immensely damaging effect upon their future welfare. It seems that the welfare needs of such children, and their future well-being and security, have simply been set aside in order to protect the traditional social structure of the family.

Section 3. The guidelines

Beyond the framework of legal controls there are the guidelines recommended by the Human Fertilisation and Embryology Authority and followed by the fertility clinics in their selection of suitable candidates for treatment. As was argued above, this amounts to a screening system for prospective parents. The Human Fertilisation and Embryology Authority guidelines follow the Human Fertilisation and Embryology Act in drawing the attention of clinics to the "welfare" of the child, "including the need of that child for a father" (Human

Fertilisation and Embryology Authority, 1993, p.13). Where a child would have no legal father, then,

> Centres are required to have regard to the child's need for a father and should pay particular attention to the prospective mother's ability to meet the child's needs throughout his or her childhood. (ibid., 1993, p.15)

The Authority therefore holds that children need fathers, and clinics must consider how that need can be met where there would be no legal father. Single or lesbian women applying for treatment must therefore be subjected to very close scrutiny by the clinics.

As was pointed out above, neither this nor Section 13 (5) of the Human Fertilisation and Embryology Act rule out single or lesbian women receiving fertility treatment as such. However, this could change. On July 8th, 1994, the Secretary of State for Health, signalled that the law and the guidelines should be tightened. In an interview on BBC Radio 4's *World at One* programme, she said that National Health Service clinics should only provide fertility treatment for married couples; she specifically targeted lesbian couples for exclusion from treatment on the NHS. She also asked the Human Fertilisation and Embryology Authority to review its guidelines covering independent clinics and their treatment of single women. She said:

> I certainly don't expect the NHS to provide infertility treatment unless there is going to be a mother and a father and, frankly, I would expect them to be married.

However, in practice, despite the "loophole" in the legal framework and the Human Fertilisation and Embryology Authority guidelines, single and lesbian women do have immense difficulty gaining access to fertility treatment because of the guidelines devised by the clinics themselves. Very few clinics will offer any sort of services for single or lesbian women. When it comes to IVF, the majority of clinics insist that people seeking treatment must be in a stable heterosexual relationship for a number of years. The restrictions on access to DI treatment are often much more severe: most clinics already meet Virginia Bottomley's demands in insisting that couples applying for DI must be married. For example, the guidelines for the University of Bristol's Centre for Reproductive Medicine say:

> For donor insemination treatment the couple should be married, because of the unusual emotional commitment required by the male partner.

The reason for such restrictions, according to the Bristol Centre's code, is the welfare of the child - treatment should not lead to adversity for any offspring. The implication here is clearly that, in the case of DI, children born to families other than married couples are at some sort of risk: unmarried heterosexual couples, same sex couples, single men and single women cannot maintain the welfare of such children as well as married heterosexuals. When it comes to IVF, only heterosexual couples can truly meet the welfare needs of such children. Again, we have the problem that the notion of "welfare" being appealed to by the argument is extraordinarily vague, such that it is not clear in what way same sex couples or single people fail to measure up, and not clear precisely what kind of risk such non-traditional families pose to children produced through fertility treatment. It is also not clear whether the claim is that only children produced through fertility treatment are at risk from non-traditional family structures, or whether all children are in danger.

John Dewar comments that this framework of control and constraint is based on the belief that "the two-parent heterosexual family is the basic unit of society" (Dewar, 1990, p.123), and he says:

> The fact that this conventional two-parent family does not exist for all children suggests that what is being defended here is not an actual social practice, but ... an "ideology of familialism"; and that central to that ideology is the preservation of a role for fathers in the upbringing of children. (ibid., p. 124)

There is a parallel with adoption practice here, in that most adoption agencies will not consider single persons as adopters of babies. The British Agencies for Adoption and Fostering advises prospective adopters:

> Most adoption agencies won't consider unmarried couples or single persons as adopters for babies... After all, the single parents who give their babies for adoption often do so because they want *two* parents for their child. (op. cit., p. 6)

However, we should note that this reason for refusing to consider single persons as adopters does not apply to the assisted conception case. And we should also note that adoption agencies are only too pleased to consider single persons as adopters when it comes to children with special needs; it is considered that single persons are often best able to meet the welfare needs of such children. An impressive amount of logical manoeuvring is needed to make this belief consistent with the claim that single persons cannot meet the welfare needs of babies.

Of course, one area of resistance against their exclusion from fertility treatment for single or lesbian women is the simplicity of the DI technique: one does not need medical or technological assistance, merely a quantity of sperm. Many single or lesbian women have used a "do-it-yourself" method. However, the legal framework has reached out to subject such families to control, through the formation (in 1993) of the Child Support Agency. Single women with children who claim welfare must now identify the father of the children, so that the State can extract financial support from him; the refusal to do so, unless risk of violence can be proved, leads to the withholding of benefit. Anonymous donors to fertility clinics are exempt from this ruling, but men who donate their sperm to women through private arrangements, rather than through a clinic, are liable under the CSA's guidelines. This affects any lesbian couples on state benefit, even where both women have been granted equal parental rights by the courts under the 1989 Children Act.

Section 4. Families without fathers

We have seen, then, that the legal framework, the Human Fertilisation and Embryology Authority guidelines, and the fertility clinics themselves, disapprove of fatherless families and actively discourage them. And if Secretary of State for Health's comments reported above indicate a future change in policy, then both the legal framework and the guidelines may be tightened to squeeze out single and lesbian women altogether. We have seen that the claim is that fatherless families cannot meet the welfare needs of children as well as children with fathers. The evidence for this is supposed to be the correlation between the rise in crime over the past 30 years and the rise in number of single-parent families. However, the move from pointing out the correlation to claiming that there is a significant connection between the two is deliberately over-simplistic and opportunistic. The most thorough and in-depth studies of crime and the family cast severe doubt on any connection between single-parenthood and crime (see Utting et al 1993).

To understand what is happening, we need to subject the argument itself to close scrutiny, and also examine the political background to the current debate about single-parent families. The first move in the argument is to claim that single-parent families, where the father is absent, cannot meet the welfare needs of children as well as two-parent families in which children receive the attention of a caring and nurturing father-figure during the most important years of their lives, especially late childhood and early adolescence. As a very general claim, this is difficult to argue against: in general, two parents are better than one, bearing in mind that it depends on who the parents in question are. But this is purely a matter of financial resources: there is no reason why a single person could not care for their children as adequately as two people given the resources and support. The argument seems to be that single-parent families need state support while two-parent families do not: but even as a gross generalisation the argument is deeply flawed - all families of whatever form receive state support: the completely independent, completely private family is exceedingly rare, if not the creature of total fantasy.

The second move in the argument is to claim that the distinction between fatherless families and the traditional "moral" family amounts to the same contrast as above. But this is simply false. First, fatherless families are not necessarily single-parenting families: a number of people could be involved in parenting. Second, the "moral" family, while it is not a single-parent family, is traditionally a single-parenting family, in which the task of caring and nurturing the children falls exclusively upon the mother. There are many ways in which fathers can be absent, and in the traditional family the gender roles of mother and father are clearly laid down such that the father is, in effect, absent because he is in a workplace outside the family domain. Another feature of traditional families of a certain class is to render children absent by sending them to boarding schools. And so the contrast between single-parent families and families that enjoy the presence of two caring, nurturing parents is not the same as a contrast between fatherless families and the traditional "moral" family.

At best, the only argument worth considering here is that two parents are better than one when it comes to meeting the welfare needs of children. As has been pointed out, this depends on who the parents in question are, and there is no reason why a single person, with sufficient resources and support, cannot care for their children as well as two people. Also, even if we take the argument seriously, then the implication is that three or four or more parents would be even better, which is precisely the possibility which biotechnology raises. But this, of course, is to miss the point of the argument. The concern of the legislation is not with the number of children involved, but that one of the parents should be a heterosexual man. The claim is that children need fathers, and only heterosexual men can fulfil that role - women cannot act as father-figures and neither can gay men. The allegation is that children are at risk of harm if they do not have a heterosexual man as a father; but one might reply that many children seem to be at risk of harm if they do. Again, unless we have a clear conception of what the welfare of children amounts to, and what it is about that welfare that only heterosexual men can provide, then the suspicion has to be that we are not opposing reasoned and considered argument here, but simply outrageous prejudice.

However, if we examine the political background to the argument, we will see that there is more at stake. Joan Isaac points out that the raising of the issue of single-parent families by the British Government has to be understood in relation to the size of the Public Sector Borrowing Requirement (Isaac,

56

1994, p.175). After showing a remarkable lack of interest in the morality of the family, the Government focused on the problem when in July 1993, a government report predicted a £14 billion increase in the cost of state benefits by the end of the century (ibid., p. 187). Single-parents on benefit are a particularly soft target if welfare spending is to be kept under control, and as Isaac comments, "it has not been single parents as such but those single parents who are poor and on state support that have been in the spotlight". (ibid., p. 175).

And she says:

> Whilst some commentators and lobbyists genuinely feel that the social order of the country is under threat from the growing numbers of single parents and their uncontrollable offspring, key politicians have had the size of the PSBR underpinning their pronouncements on single-parent families. (ibid., pp. 188-9)

While the government's scope to interfere in the lifestyles of financially independent families is limited, those on state benefits can be controlled. It may be that the government feels it is entitled to make moral judgements about the lifestyles of welfare claimants on behalf of the taxpayer; or it may be that it feels it can identify soft targets for cutting back the welfare budget. Single-parent families on welfare are such a target.

Isaac concludes:

> Clearly a "double whammy" is on the cards for the single parent family with the Child Support Agency in hot pursuit of absent partners and the ground being prepared for an onslaught on state support to the single-parent. (ibid., p. 189)

She concludes,

> Today, morality in relation to the single-parent family has acquired a price ticket (ibid., p. 189).

Section 5. Conclusion

The framework of control around reproductive techniques has as its primary aim the preservation of the "moral" family with the maintenance of a particular social structure of the family even though the biological relationships within it may be radically new. It could be replied that the primary aim of the legislation is the welfare of the children produced through assisted conception, and that this can best be met by ensuring that they are born into *traditional* families. However, we have seen that at least one aspect of the law, on access to information about origins, simply sets aside the welfare of the child in favour of saving the appearance of the traditional family structure. We have also seen that the argument against alternative family structures is based upon an ill-defined notion of welfare. And it has been noted that the argument is not, in the end, concerned with the number of adults involved in parenting children, but that one of the parents must be a heterosexual man: this, we have seen, involves some outrageous and unsubstantiated claims about the inability of women or gay men to meet the parental needs of children, and some exaggerated, if not completely fantastical, claims about the caring and nurturing role heterosexual men play in traditional family structures.

If the ideology of the "moral" family, and the gender roles it establishes, is oppressive, and if we therefore need to liberate ourselves from it, then we need a radical critique of that ideology. I have not supplied one here. My point in this essay is simply that, although the developments in reproductive technology have been presented as a radical threat to the traditional family, that representation is, in an important sense, misleading. Assisted conception, as it is practised, poses no threat to the ideology of the family, and those who oppose that ideology should not look to biotechnology for any assistance in challenging it. The reproduction revolution is not a revolution in that sense. Scientists working in the field may be interested in creating radically new forms of reproductive techniques, but they are not interested in creating radically new forms of the family. Biotechnology in practice is being used to reinforce traditional social structures, by making fertility available to heterosexual couples from a particular social and class background.

We must note the extent to which these new developments, far from liberating the family, have enabled the state and its institutions to police the structure of families more closely. Derek Lee and Robert Morgan comment that the technological changes brought about by the reproduction revolution:

> serve to augment the "panoptic technology" through which nation-states are concerned with the minutest details of the lives of their citizens; states become increasingly, perhaps necessarily, more implicated in the renegotiation of some of the most familiar contours of domestic, conjugal, and affective lives. This assault is the more needful of close and careful analysis because the ideological weaponry which accompanies the technological apparatus is discretely concealed behind cloaks of scientific objectivity and moral neutrality. The changing reproductive processes offer at once opportunities for liberation and for enslavement. (Morgan and Lee, 1990, p. 2)

This seems right, except that Lee and Morgan claim that the technological developments are being portrayed as morally neutral. In fact, in the case of biotechnology, they are being portrayed as a great danger, such that they must be closely controlled by the state and its agencies. It is this portrayal that has enabled the state to use this technological power to police the family more closely than ever. The problem is presented as an issue of "social engineering" versus "nature", with biotechnology as "social engineering" threatening traditional social structures, and "nature", if left alone, preserving them. However, as always, the idea of "nature" here should be exposed. The reality is that the social engineering is being used to reinforce traditional social structures, and so preserve the "natural order" of things. Of course, this is not to say that scientific developments in the area of reproduction should not be subject to control; but we do have to be clear about what science is being controlled for in this particular case. The legal framework that controls reproductive technology has as its aim the reinforcement of the "moral" family, and the preservation of the privileged and powerful position of men as "father-figures" within such families.

Bibliography

Brazier, M. (1992), *Medicine, Patients and the Law* New Edition (Penguin Books, London).

British Agencies for Adoption and Fostering (1986), *Adopting a Child: a Guide for People Interested in Adoption* (British Agencies for Adoption and Fostering, London).

Dewar, J. (1990), "Fathers in Law? The Case of AID", in Morgan, Derek and Lee, R. G. eds *Birthrights: Law and Ethics at the Beginnings of Life* Routledge, London).

Human Fertilisation and Embryology Authority (1993), *Code of Practice* (Human Fertilisation and Embryology Authority, London).

Isaac, J (1994), "The Politics of Morality in the UK", *Parliamentary Affairs*, Volume 47 Number 2, pp175-189.

McWhinnie, A. (1986) "AID and Infertility," *Adoption and Fostering*, Volume 10 Number 1, pp.16-18.

Morgan, D. and Lee, R. G. (1990), "Is Birth Important?" in Morgan and Lee eds. *Birthrights: Law and Ethics at the Beginnings of Life*.

Morgan, D. and Lee, R. G. (1991) *Blackstone's Guide to the Human Fertilisation and Embryology Act 1990: Abortion and Embryo Research, the New Law* (Blackstone Press Ltd, Oxford).

O'Donovan, K. (1990) "What shall we tell the children?" Reflections on children's perspectives and the sexual revolution, in Morgan and Lee eds. *Birthrights: Law and Ethics at the Beginnings of Life*.

Utting, D., Bright, J. and Henricson, C., *Crime and the Family: Improving Child-rearing and Preventing Delinquency* (Family Policy Studies Centre, 1993).

4 Bound to care: Family bonds and moral necessities

Neil Pickering

Family relationships are conventionally taken as embodying primordial ties that somehow exist outside or beyond the technological and political machinations of the world ...

(Strathern, 1992, p.11)

Taken on their own, these words may suggest an account of the concept of the family in which the form the family takes is a given. The sense of given here is cashed out in terms of something lying beyond a changeable (technological and political) world. At the same time, as Strathern goes on to remind us, these ties are reflected in society and culture. In society, they may take the form of marriage, for instance.

Some ways of speaking of this dual existence may be found in a very thought provoking chapter by Brenda Almond. She argues that the bonds in our lives (including the bonds which constitute family) are of three sorts or categories. She identifies these as:

i	biological and natural
ii	legal and artificial
iii	social and voluntary

(Almond, 1991, p. 60)

Of the bonds between couples - and particularly those which are marked by marriage - she says this:

Marriage can be seen ... as an artificial means, perhaps all we have to hand, legally and socially, to shift the loose bonding of the third non-binding and voluntary category of relationships into the deep and inescapable bonding of the first. (ibid., p. 61)

However, she also notes differing possible attitudes to marriage. For instance, she says that for some, "there is a genuine possibility of divorce, while for others, the ending of a marriage, while technically and legally feasible, will never be so in intuited reality". (ibid., p. 61)

For these "others" the reality of marriage will not be found in the legal and technical themselves, for they fail to capture, and may even betray, the depth and inescapability which marriage entails for them. Almond offers the "biological and natural" as the alternative to social, legal, voluntary and artificial. This raises an interesting question as to whether or not the biological and natural can themselves contain the intuited reality of which Almond speaks.

This paper is concerned with a reality which denies the (moral) possibility of divorce (for instance and in particular), and which, more broadly, may see the family of mother, father, and (if there are any) children, as morally the only choice. (Whenever I speak of the family in what follows, I shall always have in mind this nuclear unit.) In part 1 of this paper, this reality will be explored in three sections. In the first, "natural families and moral necessities", an argument concerning the biological will be considered. Biology will be considered as a basis of the inescapability, and will be rejected. In the second, "liberal and utopian responses", an account which seems opposed to the idea of moral necessity will be explored. And in the third, "culture, diversity and change", some reasons will be looked at for supporting a liberal view point, but these will be found not to undermine the non-liberal position. Part 2 of the paper will consider a basis for a view which claims inescapability for itself.

Part one

Natural families and moral necessities

If there may be an intuited reality in which divorce is (morally) impossible, or in which, perhaps, no form for the family other than the nuclear family is (morally) possible, the location of that reality may be said to be in what nature (or biology) gives. An immediate challenge to that location may seem to come from history. Some historians argue that the nuclear family is a relatively recent version of "the family". Charlton (1984) reminds us of Stone's (1977) study, in which are identified three different notions of "the family" dominant at different times since 1500 in Britain. Stone argues that the modern idea of the "closed domesticated nuclear family" arises in Britain from the seventeenth century on (Charlton, 1984, p. 138). Charlton himself is interested *inter alia* in the development in France of a similar idea of the family in the later part of the eighteenth century (ibid., Chapters 7 and 8).

Rousseau (an important figure in Charlton's account) suggests, near the beginning of *The Social Contract* that:

> The most ancient of all societies and the only natural one, is that of the family. (Rousseau, 1987, p.142)

The facts of history may at first sight seem to suggest that the "closed domesticated nuclear family" cannot be an unchanging or simply given thing, delivered to us, for instance, by nature. Rather, it has apparently socially evolved into its current form in recent centuries. Rousseau might respond that we need not conclude from this that the form the family takes is entirely a cultural/historical construction - an artificiality. It may be that what has happened historically is the recovery of a natural form which had been lost, at least to those levels of society which (in Rousseau's time) hired wet-nurses to feed and servants to look after the children.

Rousseau's idea that the family is in some sense "natural" is echoed more recently. A text-book of family therapy notes:

> Family therapy can be defined as the psychotherapeutic treatment of a natural social system, the family ... (Walroad-Skinner, 1976, p. 1)

At first glance, both sources may seem to give sense to a position linking the "natural" (or given) on the one hand, and the "good", on the other. It is true that, in so far as the goodness of the form the family takes is associated directly in whole or in part with its naturalness, the goodness of the natural family will also be a given. However, neither Rousseau nor Walroad-Skinner have so far established such a direct link. They value what is natural, but not yet because it is natural.

Rousseau, however, refers to a natural bonding which he seems to assume could arise only where the mother and father were (as we might put it today) the biological or genetic parents of the child; and Almond has called our attention to the biological aspect of human bonds. But, in this paper it will be suggested that the biological cannot give the sense of inescapability which may be wanted.

Modern reproductive technologies, such as *in vitro* fertilisation (IVF), based upon a modern understanding of the biology of human reproduction, seem to offer alternatives to what previously was thought of as the inescapable biology of family life. Certainly, in Rousseau's terms, what may result from a technological intervention will not be a natural family; at least in the sense that, for instance, the genetic, carrying and nurturing mother(s) may or may not be the same person, and may or may not carry the genetic child of the nurturing father. However, this falls short of showing anyone why she should condemn the non-natural family forms, or commend the "natural" form. If this is the case, then Rousseau himself must have something other than the merely biological in mind: something moral, or ideological, may also be present.

It seems true that the cry that something - such as IVF - is "unnatural" entails that it is also bad. But, the direct and general association of goodness with the biologically given seems not to be plausible. For instance, it is widely regarded as a good thing to "subvert" at least some biological events, such as the onset and progress of disease, by means of prevention or medical cure.

It may seem that, though the general belief that what is natural is good cannot hold against this point, it may still hold in this way. It may be argued that all good interventions against nature or the biological are carried out in the name of nature. For instance, it may be acceptable to cure infertility by putting right tubal defects, thus enabling the body to function naturally (that is, as most bodies function). But, where technologies such as IVF are concerned, the aim, it may be argued, is quite different, and unacceptable. IVF and other techniques do not cure infertility, for the person (or couple) is no less infertile after the IVF than before it. These techniques artificially circumvent the condition.

But, as a general claim this seems no more secure than the first. The use of circumventing technologies against naturally caused human disabilities and diseases are common and widely accepted. Wheelchairs, for instance, are not a cure for paralysis of the legs. These general arguments that the natural is also the good seem necessarily to fail. But, then, the argument that the family is good when it is natural cannot hold either, not without the addition of some other points.

The force of these arguments (both general and particular) can be disputed (cf. O'Donovan, 1984). To the extent they *are* correct, biology seems not to give the goodness in and of itself. However, it may be that what has been appealed to here is in itself a modern and reductivist way of looking at the process of procreation (cf. O'Donovan, 1984; Crowe, 1990; Steinberg, 1990). Procreation seems, in the eyes of modern biology, to be no more than a series of discrete biological events (ovulation, fertilisation, implantation) which may take place *In vitro* or *in utero*, but which have the same basic form despite location, and which are essentially cellular and biochemical in nature. Such reductivism may be at the service of ends and arise with assumptions which are not less ideological than those which, it was suggested earlier, Rousseau may have.

Jean and Maurice Bloch, for example, comment that:

64

> ... the repeated recourse to the concept of the state of nature in the seventeenth and eighteenth centuries can be understood as representing an obvious attempt to outflank the mere historical legitimacies of states and systems of domination. (Bloch and Bloch, 1980, p.26)

Rousseau's location of the good with the natural, whatever was claimed by him (or really seemed to him) to be, was not actually independent of a pre-existing moral ideal. However, the same might be said of claims today that biology and the good are logically separate.

This argument takes further the objection to biology (equated with the natural) as containing the inescapability of which Almond (op.cit.) speaks. Since the relation of biology to the cultural and the good may itself be an embodiment of particular moral positions, an appeal to a good to be found in (so called) biological facts is misconceived; the facts are not quite so purely factual as they seem.

At the same time, it suggests that a moral position may characteristically be found in claims about how things are (for instance the relation of the form the family does take to the form it should take), as well as in claims about how things should be (for example the form the family should take).

Liberal and utopian responses

When it comes to the goodness of the natural bonds between father and mother and children, this, for Rousseau, seems to have had a basis in utility. The opening of chapter 2 of Book 1 of *The Social Contract* continues:

> Even so children remain bound to their father only so long as they need him to take care of them. As soon as the need ceases the natural bond is dissolved. ... If they continue to remain united, this no longer takes place naturally but voluntarily, and the family maintains itself only by means of convention. (op. cit., p. 142)

The effectiveness or usefulness of the naturally given nuclear family, rather than its naturalness, is here claimed as a moral reason for wanting to maintain its current form. But, an argument from the utility of the family will not necessarily support a natural or otherwise given form. Moreover, in so far as it is the utility of the form the family takes which is the principle issue, the natural form will be morally commended (if it is) because it is useful, and not because it is natural.

On this account, the good is not associated with the natural except contingently. It would follow that the moral inescapability of a certain form the family might take would necessarily bear this contingent relationship to nature. But, at least on some views, once removed from the biological sphere, the notion of moral inescapability may be undermined. I shall suggest two categories into which moral arguments for alterations (typically) to the form of the family may fall. The two categories depend on the kind of alternative which may be espoused. (I do not claim that these categories are either exhaustive or necessarily exclusive.) The first category is the liberal response, and the second the utopian response.

The liberal response to the closed, domesticated nuclear form of the family is that such a family unit is fine for those who want it, or who feel morally committed to it. It should not, according to the liberal response, be set up as the only legitimate model. I believe Paul Gregory (Gregory, 1991) is arguing from a liberal position. For instance, in a passage from his *Against Couples* he argues that the exclusivity society insists on in the relationship of a couple is a bar to the formation of new meaningful friendships by either partner. These, he argues, would be perceived as a threat to the already existing relationship; the possibility of such new friendships becomes a dilemma. He goes on:

> The obvious solution to the dilemma - the pursuit of a fresh friendship whilst retaining the old - is ruled out precisely because of the prevailing norms. (ibid., p.93)

The conclusion for Gregory would seem to be that some of the norms should be abandoned, at least in so far as they exclude other possibilities - for instance by being advanced as universals and absolutes. He is not committed to the entire overthrow even of the specific norms which may (for him) need changing, however. Retention of a particular norm (of sexual or other exclusivity, for instance) by those for whom that norm is "right", need not entail for him its abandonment by those for whom it is not.

On the other hand, the utopian response to the (claimed) unsatisfactoriness of the prevailing norm is to set up a new norm. An improved and approved form for the family is purported to do better overall than the currently generally valued one. An example would be Marge Piercy's vision in *Woman on the Edge of Time* which is commended to us by Martin Thomasson in this volume. In contrast to the liberal position outlined above, there is no suggestion here that a variety of possible family models should exist. Rather, a quite different arrangement is put forward to take the place of the current norm.

Liberal and utopian responses may share a number of analytical points. Four such points may initially be noted.

It has been suggested already that, like Rousseau, "liberals" and "utopians" are interested in the utility of the family unit to achieve or prevent certain outcomes. This is not to say that there is a commitment here to strict Utilitarian principles. Gregory, for instance, may value friendship for reasons independent of its pleasurability. In the light of this non-Utilitarian value, he may question agreements about the outcomes by which the family is to be judged: should the family be judged only by its effectiveness in child rearing? Someone else, accepting the end as being the successful rearing of children, may nevertheless raise questions about the effectiveness of the natural family to achieve this.

Two of the four points seem to follow. The first is that the form the family takes seems (perhaps necessarily) bound up with moral matters, in that it appears both to be constructed in response to norms, and to be subject to morally significant questions about its utility. The second point is that, in so far as the family is logically subject to reflection on its effectiveness, it seems to be in the same way subject to change as a response to such reflection.

Further, what is to constitute the norms for assessing an effective rearing of a child may itself be at issue. This suggests a third, slightly wider point: a picture of norms and values relevant to the family as being themselves logically subject to reflection and thereby, potentially, to change.

The fourth point, arising principally from the liberal position, is that there is perceived to be a tendency to a disjunction between personal norms, on the one hand, and societal norms, on the other, at least in the case of the form the family takes. Thus, in a liberal view point, societal norms, or, as Gregory calls them "prevailing norms", for all that they can and (perhaps) should be changed, may nevertheless in reality be a source of oppressive expectations, enforcing a uniformity in the form the family takes and in who may make up a family.

It may be that there is a still more general implication of the liberal position. The liberal seems to assume that the form the family takes is a moral matter at least in part of its utility, and it seems also to be held that change is thereby logically possible. It seems also, however, perhaps to be felt additionally that moral reflection should take place. This point is perhaps better put like this: the form the family takes *matters*, and by that is meant, in part, that it should be subjected to moral reflection.

Where Rousseau (on the one hand) and the liberal/utopian (on the other hand) disagree, then, is about the moral acceptability of change to the family; they do not disagree that this is a moral matter to be judged by moral (in this case broadly utilitarian) precepts. And further, though disagreeing morally, they are agreed that a change in moral attitudes to the form the family unit should take could not come from nature; the alternative to nature is the voluntary and the conventional (as Rousseau would put it) or the normative as the liberals would have it.

In so far as it is the hope of this paper to describe a position in which moral necessities are connected to the form the family should take, it seems that the liberal's conclusion that the form the family takes is essentially a normative and a moral matter is a significantly shared belief. However, in so far as the liberal wants also to conclude that the form of the family is thereby both logically subject to (and further, perhaps should be subject to) moral reflection and also open to the possibility of change, there is a clear difference between a liberal/utopian analysis and the opposing analysis explored in this paper.

Culture, diversity and change

So far, a sketch of a liberal/utopian analysis has been given, without much in the way of justification. The position has been taken to assume, for instance, that norms connected with the family, and judgements of the family's effectiveness are logically subject to reflection and the possibility of change. That this, in a broadly liberal view, is a feature of anything influenced chiefly by culture as opposed to nature (to accept for a moment the distinction as factual) is suggested by the range of terms which seem to fall under the notion of the cultural. Rousseau (1987) mentions the "voluntary and conventional", Almond (1991) refers to the artificial, legal, social and voluntary, and Strathern (1992) speaks of the technological and political and their "machinations".

Now, one characteristic of arrangements which are influenced by these may be said to be diversity of familial norms and familial forms. We may be pointed to the Kibbutz in Israel; to families where there are traditionally more than two parents; to the reality of the role that is played in bringing up children by grandparents, and so forth. Variety is the essence of the picture of the human family (it may be observed).

The mere existence of diversity in the form the family takes does not seem to show, however, that it is culture which underlies it, and not nature. Rather, it may be argued, cultural diversity itself is natural (however ideologically useful it might seem to be to deny it). Without attempting to adjudicate on this complex matter, it may still be possible to draw two points out of the differences which make it up.

First, diversity, however it may arise, may suggest to someone that no one form the family takes could be morally necessitated or inescapable. Diversity suggests (moral) choice, on this account. This point will be carried forward, and a response will be suggested to it in the latter part of this paper.

Second, it may still be argued that cultural diversity chiefly represents the result of genuine human agency, in so far as moral norms are taken to be part of culture. What is objectionable about the kind of explanation which the word "biological" suggests goes with the form(s) which the family takes, then, might be that it entails a mechanistic, deterministic, and causal link between a person's (human) nature and those forms. That is, "biological" seems to deny to human individuals a sense of moral agency in, or commitment to, the very values which may be said to oblige them to reflect upon the form the family should take.

This concern about the meaning of biological accounts of human motivation is one which the point of view chiefly to be explored in this paper and the liberal point of view may equally share. The inescapability of a moral view point looks unlikely to be captured by reductivist accounts, by the very same token of genuine human agency which the liberal appeals to.

Part two

Almond (1991) wants to construe the family as based around what she claims factually to be a non-biological tie, yet still to speak of the inescapable. At the "heart" of the family, as Almond puts it is the couple; but their coming together is not determined by biology at all[1].

> The quintessential network of bonding is the family, and at the heart of *that* system, the nuclear family, lies a central relationship between two people which, unlike all other family relationships, is *not* based on a biological or blood tie - it is not natural but created, whether by the will of the two people themselves, or, in some cases, by external agencies or circumstantial constraints. (ibid., p. 60, original emphasis)

Professor Almond's notions of depth and inescapability in the marriage tie imply something more than can be contained by the legal, though what is implied might in some sense be expressed through such an artificial institution. Marriage, though it may also be a legal procedure, is more than a legal contract, then. The inescapability of marriage may be expressed in the words, "Whom God hath joined, let no man put asunder"; and in vows referring to staying together, "for richer, for poorer, in sickness and in health, 'til death us do part". Yet, these words are spoken, and perhaps in some sense meant, by many, who later have extra-marital sex, or divorce.

A vow, or a promise, or an institution such as marriage, may, however, play a role in someone's life just because it rests upon and sets up expectations, feelings and responses which the person holds inescapably. In the following four sections, this basis for an account of the moral inescapability of marriage for some individuals and groups will be explored. In the first section, "responses and gut reactions", arguments based upon the unbidden nature of certain feelings will be considered. In the second, "necessity and moral agency", an objection concerning the role of human moral agency will be considered and responded to. In the third section, the role of ideology and philosophy in a wider analysis of the morally inescapable will be taken up, and a brief fourth section ("excluding other possibilities") will conclude the paper.

Responses and gut reactions

For some, entering certain institutions, such as marriage, may involve the necessary setting up of expectations. Even where the expectations of marriage may be implicit, responses may arise unbidden where they are not fulfilled. An example from *Wild Swans* (Jung Chang, 1993) comes to mind here. The example involves responses to pressures upon the traditional form of the family. Having briefly given the example, this section of the paper will consider a number of objections to the account of the role of what will be described initially as unbidden responses.

The author's mother (named De-hong) marries a man (Shou-yu) who is a member of the communist party of China. In a series of incidents, Shou-yu's communist purity and the expectations of his wife come into conflict. For example, he refuses to give De-hong a lift in his jeep, or even to carry anything for her, during one long journey they make with other sympathizers of communism and officials of the party. She has therefore to accomplish the journey entirely on foot, despite being exhausted, and vomiting frequently (she later turns out to have been pregnant) (ibid., pp. 191-192).

Her husband's attitude to her during a subsequent pregnancy embitters De-hong. But here she also calls his attention to the natural tie he has with the unborn baby, "reminding" him, when he tries to prevent De-hong's mother cooking her any special food, that the child she is carrying is his as well as hers (ibid., p. 216).

The writer records how, on one occasion, Shou-yu's lack of sympathy for his wife (and indeed for his child) causes her to ask for a divorce - whereupon Shou-yu vows to be a better husband in the future. The responses of De-hong are moral in character, at least, in these two senses. Shou-yu's failures (as De-hong might see them) are significant failures in the light of the special connection she believes to exist in the nature of the relationship which Shou-yu has with her and their child; and her resentment and unhappiness requires of Shou-yu that he promise to be a better husband in the future.

It has been suggested that one way in which there may be an inescapability here is in the way in which these responses arise unbidden in De-hong. Importantly, too, the failures seem significant, a fact which is registered and embodied in language and feelings taking moral form. The unbidden response, to something which matters, when verbalised, may have the form

70

"he must (or should) treat his wife/child better". It will be important to this exploration, ultimately, to see that the unbidden nature of the response and the form the response takes may come together.

Taking the idea of unbidden responses on its own, however, may seem to fail to give the right kind of inescapability. To say these responses arise unbidden for De-hong, may imply a form of gut reaction which the person cannot help but have. But the notion of a gut reaction or response may suggest something biological. At the very least, the emphasis on what cannot be helped may seem to give a picture of De-hong's moral life with a weak notion of moral agency.

This is not to argue that a moral life must be more than gut reactions and responses. But, there are several reasons for wanting to say more.

First, much of what we may call moral life certainly seems to consist of more than unbidden responses. People reflect morally upon their actions, speak of and perhaps have beliefs, knowledge, and opinion connected to their actions and reactions. Certainly De-hong and Shou-yu do reflect, even in the midst of their emotions and feelings. A liberal may further suggest, the characteristic of a reflective moral life is that changes may be made in beliefs, and actions, at least in this sense: moral reflection includes reflection upon not only the character of what is (the given), but also what *ought* to be. It was suggested earlier that the liberal as construed in this paper, sees an obligation to reflection where the form the family takes is at issue.

Second, we may want to say more if gut reactions seem to give a picture of a person as passively "in the grip" of certain reactions and responses. Such a picture may seem not to fit well with personal commitment or agency, in the sense that the person has no control over such reactions. If some account of agency of this kind is necessary to a plausible account of moral inescapability, then the necessity or inescapability here seems once more to be of the wrong sort.

Third, more may need to be added even supposing that gut reactions are in some way important to moral life. Though they may be important, it may not follow that they can plausibly be said to constitute or be part of moral life. Speaking of one response which might be called "gut", jealousy, Gregory notes how jealousy may seem to justify exclusivity in relations between couples. But he argues:

> Is it not nearer the truth to say that the traditional norms encourage and justify jealousy? ... people feel themselves to be morally in the right to feel jealousy; the ethic of exclusivity tells them that they have a right to an exclusive claim on their partner. (op. cit., p. 93)

For Gregory, then, jealousy is not justificatory; rather it is in need of justification (and it does indeed receive that justification from traditional norms). The point is that jealousy seems to have no foundational place internal to morality. And it may be claimed that this is a feature of gut reactions generally.

Moreover, as Shou-yu seems to demonstrate, by dint of personal involvement in a revolution of a sufficiently far reaching nature, a cultural revolution if you like, one can come to take principles other than those which may arise unbidden, as one's guides in life. However powerful the traditional importance of family may have been, even for Shou-yu himself, he is both able, and perhaps feels morally obliged, to resist some unbidden responses, at least in certain situations. They become, on this account, temptations, to be resisted in the light of higher moral values. But now, a person's moral agency seems not to include gut reactions and unbidden responses; they may lie beyond it, subject to its judgement.

Necessity and personal human agency

An alternative account, even of gut reactions like jealousy, perhaps, is that they may bring their own justification with them; likewise, De-hong's resentment and sense of abandonment at her treatment by Shou-yu may be self justifying. This might make sense if we describe her resentment in these terms: it is resentment at his lack of sympathy, where his sympathy was an expectation, and his actions are seen as lacking sympathy. This is to suggest that her resentment, or her sense of abandonment, are not merely free floating feelings, but that they arise in and partly constitute the reality of her expectations and what subsequently happened to her. In this account, then, there is not necessarily room for a distinction between the gut reaction of resentment and the justification. The "justification" might have come from an independent account of reality, but De-hong's reality is here part of the description of the resentment.

It may be argued also that this account is not necessarily one which entails an absence of personal human agency. It may, on the other hand, raise a question about what such agency may or must amount to in someone's life, and how it may or must be described. Speaking of how a gut reaction or unbidden response to an event and the justification of such a reaction by that event may come together; someone may want to speak here of a realisation of, or grasping of, the reality of a situation, or of the true meaning of a situation. On this account we may speak of De-hong not merely reacting to a situation, but of her grasping its significance. Such an account seems to be one which entails personal human agency, on the one hand, and some sense of necessity or inescapability on the other. She grasps or apprehends the reality or the truth of what has happened.

Or, we might say, that she is grasped by ("struck by") the meaning, or the truth of what has happened. This, however, is not an account which entails utter human passivity: responses or gut-reactions construed in terms of being grasped by or grasping the meaning or truth of a situation cannot plausibly be reduced, for instance, to a biological account.

Even in the case of jealousy which Gregory brings to our attention, the jealousy arises out of circumstances which are somewhat complex in character (the couple are married, for instance). Thus, though jealousy may seem a primordial reaction, it is in this case bound up with the social expectations and realities which marriage embodies. A description of De-hong's unbidden responses may include not only the idea that it is a gut reaction, but also that it is a response to complex social set of expectations and realities which marriage entails for her. Likewise, Almond's is a claim about an intuited reality in the case of the possibility of divorce, which one could not have without an idea of marriage. Further, these, are moral reactions and responses, in that they are partly constitutive of a moral context. They cannot be described in terms only of the biological.

Thus, gut reactions may be at once primordial, or even apparently natural, and at the same time deeply bound up with the person as a member of society and of a particular culture. Further, human reflection on the moral may start from and fall back upon such responses; they may be properly part of moral reflectivity, and not a precursor to it, or in any way beyond it, and thereby necessarily subject to its independent judgement.

Ideology and philosophy

But now it may be argued that an unacceptably limited notion of moral reflection is being used. While someone may, as a matter of fact, not get beyond such starters and stoppers, they are not logically beyond further philosophical reflection and characterisation.

Briefly, here, I will reflect on two relations which may be said to hold between philosophical analysis and personal moral stoppers and starters in the form of gut-reactions. The first entails the idea that philosophy can offer some analytical stance from which all moral view points would be equally valid and similarly characterised. Such a standpoint would seem to leave room for the undermining of the sense someone within such a moral view point might have, that his or her view point was the "only" or the "right" one, and, if you like, inescapable or necessary in that sense.

Here the idea might be that a human construct - perhaps "ideology" - is a determining factor in the idea that (for instance) the family must or should take a certain form. That is to say, that it is only from a within a particular ideological view point that anything like that can appear to be grasped. Thus,

Rousseau, who may be tempted to argue that the good form of the family is unchanging and inescapable, would appear to be working within a particular ideological framework. A modern example, with deep historical roots, might be that of the Roman Catholic Church. And of such frameworks two things may be claimed. First, that it is they that give the impression, if anything does, that things are as they must and should be in respect of the particular form the family should take. Second, that these frameworks, are themselves susceptible to moral criticism and to change.

But, it is not clear what must follow from this. As with a possible liberal distinction between societal norms and individual values, a picture may be appealed to here in which ideology lies outside individuals, in this sense: that it forms them in its own image, perhaps from birth. And that may seem to imply that ultimately, any person can (logically) become aware of this, and, having done so, judge for herself that she wants or does not want to continue with this ideological framework. At a non-abstract level, such a revolution in thought may seem to be happening, to different degrees, in people like Shou-yu.

It is not the intention of this paper to deny that this analytical level may exist, at least in some sense. For instance, Shou-yu has found a (communist) framework from which to look at traditional Chinese values concerning the family, and show them to be ideological - for instance created in order to uphold a corrupt system of nepotism. Further, the ideals of communism in China may appear to Shou-yu as incontrovertibly the right ones. That is, to characterise the role communism plays in his eyes, it would not be sufficient to call it another ideology equal analytically - or morally - with the rest. For him, then, communism is the standpoint referred to.

But, in so far as it is also a moral standpoint, a stand point which makes available a moral assessment of an ideology, it will itself have to contain values by which such an assessment could be made. If, on the other hand, it merely suggested that all moral view points were ideological in character, nothing moral would seem to follow for any view point.

We may then deny either that an analytical objectivity which is beyond all systems of (moral) belief and particular beliefs necessarily exists for everyone, or that it has moral relevance if it could be found. But such denials need not be end of the matter.

> ... to see differently ... for once, to *want* to see differently, is no small discipline and preparation of the intellect for its future "objectivity" - the latter understood not as "contemplation without interest" (which is a nonsensical absurdity), but as the ability *to control* one's Pro and Con and to dispose of them, so that one knows how to employ a variety of perspectives and affective interpretations in the service of knowledge. (Nietzsche, 1989, p. 119, original emphasis)

Nietzsche here argues that there is no "view from nowhere" - as Nagel might put it (Nagel, 1986)[2]; that all views show an interest. If such interest may include the moral, then, for Nietzsche, to that extent we cannot abandon all moral outlooks. But, for Nietzsche we may control our "Pro and Con". This may perhaps mean we may alter our moral view so as to see things with a different moral weighting; or indeed, and more radically, to see the notion of moral pro and con itself in different ways.

It is perhaps unconventional, and even somewhat perverse, to link Nietzsche to a liberal outlook. To achieve this unusual feat would entail interpreting this passage as an appeal to grasp things from positions (in ways) which are not your own way. In that sense, it may be an appeal which would win liberal backing, in seeming to be a necessary first step to tolerance of variety and diversity, and encouragement of those seeking ways which lie outside the norms of a particular ideology, culture, religion, or society.

Excluding other possibilities

However, unless Nietzsche has it in mind that we should become other people, it cannot be that trying to grasp things as others grasp them will necessarily lead to agreement with their views, or even tolerance of them. All that may be grasped, for some, is the horror of the other view. For others, even the attempt to see from other standpoints may be immoral.

This paper has been exploring a view of the form the family should take. The view explored involves the idea that the domesticated, nuclear family is a morally inescapable form. Earlier, where the liberal/utopian position was being considered, it was asserted that diversity suggests choice. But, where one form of the family may be said to be morally inescapable, such a choice seems not to exist. Now that rejection of choice can be characterised more fully. First, even where it might make sense to speak of understanding or grasping things as others grasp them, that need not entail finding in what has been grasped, a choice for oneself; one may rather have seen a path to destruction. Second, it may be that certain view points on the form the family must take, can be the sort of view points they are, only in excluding other possibilities. This is to argue that, for such view points, the sense of inescapability will be partly expressed in their claim to be the only possible moral view.

This may, further, entail a view (from within the moral view point) on the nature of the moral itself: that it is a given, an unalterable, perhaps coming from beyond the ken of the person, and perhaps winning the person's allegiance hands down, yet, and at the same time, grasped by the person for herself. Almond's "intuited reality" in which divorce is not a possibility may (on the account given here) be a moral reality excluding all other possibilities.

That marriage has been ordained as the mode in which people may cohabit and reproduce, that the relationship of marriage is exclusive of other sexual liaisons, these may seem to some fully meaningful only as absolutes and universals. But, for instance, we have construed 'Pro' and '

For anyone taking the position explored in this paper, the liberal appeal for a diversity of moral norms in the form the family takes, and for (individual) choice within that diversity, said to be made available by the possibility of reflection and perhaps change, may seem to reveal a lack of sensitivity to the reality. But for a liberal, as I have construed him or her, the moral force of the appeal to reflection and all that may follow from it, may itself be inescapable.

Notes

1. It might be objected that there is a sufficient biological explanation of the tie, if we take seriously talk of the chemistry of attraction and so forth. But for reasons already given, I would want to reject such reductivism.

2. The intention is not to imply here that Nagel holds that there is a moral "view from nowhere".

Acknowledgement

I would like to thank Brenda Almond and Carole Ulanowsky for encouraging me to write this paper and Don Evans and Carole Ulanowsky for their clarifying comments on it; only I am responsible for what has finally resulted.

Bibliography

Almond, B. (1991), "Human Bonds" in Almond, B. and Hill, D. (eds), *Applied Philosophy Morals and Metaphysics in Contemporary Debate*, Routledge, London.

Bloch, M. and Bloch, J. H. (1980), "Women and the Dialectics of Nature in Eighteenth Century French Thought" in MacCormack, C. P. and Strathern, M. (eds), *Nature, Culture and Gender*, Cambridge University Press, Cambridge.

Charlton, D.G. (1984), *New Images of the Natural in France A Study in European Cultural History 1750-1800*, Cambridge University Press, Cambridge.

Crowe, C. (1990), "Whose mind over whose matter? Women *in vitro* fertilisation and the development of scientific knowledge" in McNeil, M. Varcoe, I. and Yearley, S. (eds), *The New Reproductive Technologies*, MacMillan, Basingstoke and London.

Gregory, P. (1991), "Against Couples" in Almond, B. and Hill, D. (eds), *Applied Philosophy Morals and Metaphysics in Contemporary Debate*, Routledge, London.

Jung Chang (1993), *Wild Swans Three Daughters of China*, Flamingo, London.

Nagel, T. (1986), *View From Nowhere* Oxford University Press, Oxford.

Nietzsche, F. Transl. Kaufmann, W. and Hollingdale, R.J. (1989), "On the Genealogy of Morals" in Kaufmann, W. (ed.), *On the Genealogy of Morals and Ecce Homo*, Vintage Books, New York.

O'Donovan, O. (1984), *Begotten or Made?* Oxford University Press, Oxford.

Piercy, M. (1979), *Woman on the Edge of Time* Women's Press, London.

Rousseau, J-J., (1987) "On the Social Contract." Cress, D.A., (ed.) (1987) in *The Basic Political Writings of Jean-Jacques Rousseau* Hackett Publishing Company, Indianapolis. USA.

Steinberg, D. L. (1990), "The depersonalisation of women through the administration of *in vitro* fertilisation" in McNeil, M. Varcoe, I. and Yearley, S. (eds), *The New Reproductive Technologies*, MacMillan, Basingstoke and London.

Strathern, M. (1992), *After Nature. English Kinship in the Late Twentieth Century*, Cambridge University Press, Cambridge.

Thomasson, M. (1995), "A very wise child? Marge Piercy and the Radical Feminist Utopia" in Ulanowsky, C. E. (ed.) *The Family in the Age of Biotechnology* Avebury, Aldershot.

Walroad-Skinner, S. (1976), *Family Therapy: The Treatment of Natural Systems*, Routledge and Kegan Paul, London.

5 A very wise child – ectogenesis and the biological family

Martin Thomasson

Marge Piercy's *Woman on the Edge of Time*, (Piercy, 1979) is the story of Connie, a poverty-stricken, Hispanic American woman, who, through a conspiracy of circumstances, finds herself committed to an asylum. Whilst interned, she experiences the first of a series of visitations from Luciente, a woman from the future who teaches Connie to transport herself - mentally - into the future, where she visits Luciente's community at a place called Mattapoisett.

Mattapoisett is Piercy's utopian vision of a community in which technology is used reflectively and caringly to enhance the lives of its inhabitants. A central theme of the novel is, then, a contrast between technology in our time - as a powerful tool of control exercised by an elite - and its application in Luciente's community as a tool for the enrichment of all. Luciente serves as our guide to a world full of radical social and technological arrangements, whilst Connie plays Devil's Advocate, voicing the outrage and the fears that the reader might well experience when confronted with a world which challenges so many of our assumptions whilst simultaneously presenting itself as a distinct improvement on contemporary western society.

Central to the education that Connie receives through Luciente's guidance is the Mattapoisett community's use of technology to re-invent the family. Children are produced ectogenetically and are raised by three "comothers" (who may be male or female), none of whom are genetically linked to the child. Whilst the comothers are granted primary responsibility for rearing the child to puberty, their responsibility is not exclusive, the belief being that child-rearing is a communal task.

Piercy's construction of the Mattapoisett community raises many important and fascinating questions about the family, only some of which can be tackled in this paper. My focus here will be on two issues which the prospect of ectogenesis requires us to confront concerning the function and value of human bonding.

The first is the question of what a child has to gain from being raised by its biological parents. We should probably say that, in the ideal case, a child's parents will assume responsibility for her welfare; be committed to providing her with a stable environment (perhaps via their commitment to each other); will form a deep and intimate bond with her (which will last for the rest of their lives), and will give her a sense of belonging necessary for her to be emotionally secure.

I shall examine these four elements: responsibility, commitment, intimacy and belonging - though not entirely separately since they are, themselves, intimately linked.

Throughout, I shall refer to and seek to provide a critique of a phenomenon which I call "one-to-oneness", by which I mean that feature of human bonding as we experience it which is premised upon exclusivity. At bottom, one-to-oneness is the central issue of this paper - whether exclusivity in bonding offers us special benefits for which a broader network of bonds could offer neither replacement nor compensation.

> A little boy - three or four years old - goes to his mother. "Mummy," he asks, "Where did I come from?" Not being very "modern", his mother cringes internally, shifts from one foot to the other and then answers, "Well, darling,.. your Daddy and I found you under a stone in the garden". The little boy thinks about this for a while, and then goes out into the garden and starts turning over rocks. Eventually, he turns over a big, flat rock and underneath it he finds a frog. He grabs the frog, examines it closely, and then he says to it, "Well, you're an ugly little beggar, but I love you, 'cause I'm your Daddy."

Bad joke or not, I think this story says something important about our view of biological parenting. What it speaks of is *unconditional love*. Your Daddy (and your Mummy too) will love you, no matter what you look like and, by implication, no matter how you shape up in other respects, and this, it is commonly held, is because your parents are responsible for your existence in a biological sense. This biological bond is thought to generate a commitment from your parents to you which creates an especially intimate bond. (An interesting feature of the joke is that, of course, the little boy and the frog are *not* linked in this way. What matters here, so it seems, is the child's *beliefs* in tandem with *cultural expectations*.) This belief in the unconditional love of biological parents for their children is certainly open to challenge. However, let us, for the sake of argument, allow that biological parents, by and large, *do* offer their children this benefit. Such a concession need not win the day for biological parents over the elective parents of the Mattapoisett community, however, for against this alleged plus there are many negatives which must be weighed in the balance before we can reach a final decision.

We often speak of children as belonging to their (biological) parents. It is time to say that there is a sense of belonging that is closely akin to notions of home, of rightness of place, of a special bonding - indeed of a certain kind of intimacy. We speak in this respect of people belonging together in a way that suggests a completeness not dissimilar to the idea of completeness postulated in the *Symposium* by Aristophanes. This, however, is not generally what we intend when we speak of a child belonging to her parents. If I speak of a child belonging to me, I am generally claiming rights to make decisions about her life, whilst simultaneously implying that others (including the child herself) are properly to be excluded from making such decisions. At the same time, I am asserting the existence of a bond between myself and this child (a bond of belonging, of ownership) to the exclusion of other children (c.f. Hearn, 1987, pp.156-158).[2] In this sense, the nuclear/biological family is quite clearly alienating, as it tends to set one unit up against another, making (to adapt Marx) enemies and competitors of those who could be friends and collaborators. Similar effects can be seen in the development of certain forms of nationalism - where a national identity is often premised on a notion of belonging defined only in outline against a background of exclusion. Being "one of us" in the nationalist context thus becomes a "negative" concept, given form largely, if not solely, by reference to those who are *not* "one of us". To return to the family context, what matters about being biologically "one of us" is that we can enhance family unity by implicit reference to some threat posed by those who are not "one of us" i.e., not family.

In this respect, a concept of belonging which is broader and less rigid - such as we find in the Mattapoisett community - must of its nature be less prone to exclusionary tendencies, to fear and condemnation of the alien *Other* and hence more amenable to difference in a positive sense.

Biological belonging cannot escape the suggestion of the child as property of the parent.[3] In so far as I am your property (I belong to you), the responsibility for my actions, for my well-being devolves upon you, rather than residing entirely within me.[4] When we think of a child "belonging" to her parents, we think of them as being responsible for her in these ways. This responsibility, on the biological model has to be exclusive, since there can, at most, only be two biological parents.

There are several consequences of this, each of which seems to speak in favour of the Mattapoisett community, at the expense of the nuclear/biological family.

The first consequence is the burden of responsibility placed upon the biological parents - a burden which I would suggest leads to protective rather than supportive parenting. By this I mean that biological parents being, as it were, alone in the world, tend to conduct themselves with an eye to avoiding mistakes, rather than contemplating what we might call "creative parenting". This timidity leads to a fear of experimentation - indeed the very idea of experimenting with our child's upbringing strikes us as immoral and irresponsible. (This appears especially true in current times, when we are, as a society, more ready to criticize parental failure than to offer understanding and support to parents in difficulty.) Another manifestation of this fear is a desire to control all aspects of our child's life (under the guise of protection).[5]

The second consequence, which also involves control, is a tendency towards possessiveness. This is *my* child, linked to me by blood and, in the case of the mother, via the work and the pain of pregnancy and childbirth.

Possessiveness also results from the third consequence of the exclusionary nature of biological parenting, which is that parenting has for us a *gender-defining role*. That is, one becomes a "complete" man in our society by fathering a child, a complete (real) woman by giving birth. In the case of the woman, given her usual role in child-rearing, motherhood becomes a life-defining activity - Luciente points this out to Connie (Piercy, 1979, p.251).

The possessiveness that results from these factors leads to an unwillingness to let go, to allow the child to assume responsibility for her own life (as does the fear of failing caused by the excessive burden of responsibility for the biological parent). Again, control plays a part here, hence the strict separation of adult and child worlds (particularly when it comes to sexuality). This, of course, all has the effect of inhibiting the development of the child into an autonomous being (which, from the child's point of view, is what parenting ought to be about). The concept of responsibility here is very interesting. We say that children are not responsible, but how does one become responsible ? Most usually, by being allowed to take responsibility. But we can't allow the child to take responsibility until she shows she can behave responsibly. And so on, with a debilitating circularity. For this is not just a Catch 22, it is also a self-fulfilling prophesy. What better way to foster irresponsibility in another than to take upon yourself ultimate responsibility for their actions ? This communicates to the other both that she is incapable of acting responsibly, and also that she need not concern herself with trying to assume responsibility since the burden of her errors will always be borne by you.

The next consequence of exclusive biological parent responsibility is the creation of fear in the child. The deliberate fostering of exclusive dependency on the parent(s) must lead to a fear of loss: an acute fear of the death or desertion of a parent. Moreover, this dependence must incline the child to excessive fear of parental displeasure (c.f. Freud's view of child development). Both of these fears (of loss and of incurring displeasure) are emphasized by the biological pair-bond, since any dispute between parents must leave the child with a fear of loss through desertion and the added fear of incurring the displeasure of one parent by being perceived as taking sides. The Mattapoisett arrangement offers interesting options in two senses. Firstly, Comothers are not lovers, therefore not prone to "love misunderstandings" as Luciente puts it. Secondly, having three parents instead of two creates an interesting emotional mathematics, since in the usual case where there are two parents in dispute, whichever way the child jumps will create an imbalance combined with the knowledge that jumping the other way would have created the opposite imbalance [2:1 or 1:2]. In this context, the child's intervention can be perceived (especially by the child) as decisive. With three parents however, the child's stance is less dramatic, in that it either confirms what has already been decided [changing 2:1 to 3:1] or creates a balance [2:1 to 2:2]. In addition to all of this, the Mattapoisett community offers parental support on a communal level, which could be of critical, if secondary, importance.

Another consequence of our model of biological parenting seems to me to set us up for one-to-oneness in our sexual relationships. That is, it persuades us that our goal should be to invest ourselves in a single, all-consuming relationship. I have one mother, one father; they have one husband, one wife (I am fully aware that many western families do not fit this pattern; the point is that the deviations are almost invariably subsets of this pattern, often with express intent to mimic the pattern as nearly as possible). Such a model could be said to saddle us with the goal of finding this *one other* (*our other half* as Aristophanes quite literally describes it, in *the Symposium*) who will be the answer to our dreams, solve all our problems, fill the emptiness - in the way that our parents do (or are supposed to do). I will say no more than that this urge to unload responsibility for ourselves strikes me as the worst kind of Sartrean *bad faith*. Moreover, when it doesn't work (as it very often doesn't) it leaves us with a sense of failure, perhaps even of blame. That is, the failure to achieve the ideal manifests itself either as our own fault (due to some character flaw), our partner's fault, or as the "world's". In other words, we lack a sense of proportion in responsibility - either we assume total responsibility (like the parent) or we totally renounce responsibility (like the child). In any event, we persist in describing the failure as individual or as belonging to a whole sex ("this is the way men are"). We never seem to recognise it for what it is: a failure of a system.

All of these problems seem to me to stem not merely from the pair-bond system and its resolution under capitalism into isolated, boxed-in family units, but also of the valourizing of the biological family that goes with it. All of these must be weighed against the (putative) unconditional love of the biological parent for her/his child. In all of these respects, I think the Mattapoisett community offers the more optimistic and humane options.

However, there are questions that should be raised about the non-biological, networking approach to child-rearing. The most pressing of these concern commitment and intimacy.

Whilst the decision to become a biological parent is often a matter of choice, once that decision "bears fruit", there is no retraction. One may refuse the commitment (refuse to act upon one's responsibility), but a biological link is one that cannot be rescinded. In part, it is the irrevocable nature of this link that furnishes our confidence in the commitment of the biological parent when compared to the elective commitment of the Mattapoisett comother or other "adoptive" parent. We may, in our minds, compare the institution of marriage in the days before divorce was an acceptable option, with the state of marriage today. It could from this be argued that the very fact that divorce is now an option undermines the commitment of the partners and makes them too ready to terminate the arrangement, whereas, when there was no such option, problems were overcome simply because they *had* to be overcome. In just this way, where parents *choose* to be parents of a non-biological kind, might they not also show a greater readiness to renounce that decision when difficulties present themselves - being more inclined to accept that they made the wrong choice than to see the problems through to a solution? In this sense, it might appear that biological parenting offers the better alternative in that, because the child belongs in a *biological* way, the parents are less prone to consider withdrawing their commitment.

Several responses can be made to this. Firstly, adoptive parents are not inevitably (nor perhaps even characteristically) prone to withdraw their commitment to their children. Secondly, it is conceivable that, given the social arrangements in the Mattapoisett community, withdrawal from parenting by choice might well not be so traumatic an experience as it is in our society. Thirdly, choice here works both ways; the child can also elect to change parents (I do not wish to consider here whether, as an issue of autonomy, this is a good or a bad thing, only to observe that it is not self-evidently bad). Finally, in the Mattapoisett community we are dealing with three parents instead of two. If one parent were to withdraw, two would remain and a third could be co-opted by agreement. If two parents were lost, one at least would remain. As for the extreme possibility, one can only guess at what Lady Bracknell would have to say of a child who lost *three* parents ! From all this, I conclude that commitment does not weigh heavily in favour of biological parenting.

But what of intimacy? Surely the biological, paired family wins out here. It can be argued that a genuine intimacy requires that we restrict the scope of our bonding and focus on the other person in a very particular way. In other words, it might be said that true intimacy requires precisely that one-to-oneness I have so far criticised and sought to undermine.

It certainly seems to be undeniable that the development of intimacy requires time and effort, both in its establishment and in its maintenance. It also seems to require a certain degree of exclusivity in that it would seem that what makes my bond with X special (i.e. intimate) is that I exclude most (or even all) others from the "gifts" that I share with X. In this way, it seems that the setting up of boundaries which exclude others facilitates intimacy by creating a sense of security and specialness. In fact, it could be argued that the kind of "networking" of bonds shown in the Mattapoisett community is a kind of emotional cowardice, indicating a refusal to bond deeply with a single other, which is really due to the fear that they might leave or die.

Jeffrey Reiman offers some interesting perspectives on this, pointing out that the exclusionist account given above, "suggests a market conception of personal intimacy". (Reiman 1977, p.32.) In contrast, Reiman argues that what counts in intimacy is not what you share but the spirit in which you share it. In other words, intimacy is not some form of capital whose value is dependent on you having it while others don't. That we tend to treat it this way may say more about current social conditions (competition etc) than about the *nature* of intimacy. My capacity for intimacy will certainly be conditional upon factors such as time and energy, and by other factors more particular to my own nature (such as patience and gregariousness), but none of these imply one-to-oneness.

Beyond this, there seems to me to be a case to be argued that one-to-oneness actually inhibits the growth of intimacy in two ways. First, the reliance on a *single* other may engender an exaggerated fear of rejection or loss.[6] Second, as Reiman argues, the connection between privacy and intimacy lies not in the erecting of barriers of privacy around the partners in *intimacy* (thereby including "us" only by excluding "them"), but in establishing the boundaries of the self. In other words, the significance of privacy (exclusion) to intimacy lies in *choice*. Privacy allows me to choose *whether* to share and *with whom*. One-to-oneness tends towards an exaggerated and invasive proximity - whether it be between lovers or between biological parent and child - wherein any boundaries of privacy the child or loved one may wish to erect (or leave unbreached) tend to be viewed with suspicion, as some form of potential or actual betrayal. This can be equally true whether we are dealing with the issue of keeping something for ourselves (e.g. choosing not to reveal some secret desire) or of sharing with one who is outside the pair bond (witness, for example, the conflict experienced by many in trying to maintain old friendships in the face of new love affairs, and also the jealousy often expressed between parent and lover or spouse.)

Reiman argues that, in order to be truly intimate, people need to develop (and maintain) a sense of self, so that they may freely choose to give themselves. This development can only happen in a private space (a space of one's own), yet one-to-oneness mitigates against the construction of such a space. In contrast, The Mattapoisett community is predicated on personal space and in this way *facilitates* intimacy. So, contrary to first appearances, the issue of intimacy may actually weigh against biological parenting.

Biological families *can* provide wonderful nurturing environments for children and life-enhancing experiences for their parents. My intention here has not been to devalue this, but rather to show the good fortune and heroism that successful parenting in a paired, biological context requires, whilst suggesting that a non-biological, ectogenetic form of parenting could provide the same and greater rewards for both child and parent without demanding such superhuman qualities.

There has been much talk about the promise - and perhaps even more about the threat - of biotechnology. The bulk of the discussion has seemed to me to focus on the possible consequences for the biological individual, ignoring, for the most part, its potential impact on the social group. In this paper, I have sought to redress the balance by considering some of the ways in which the options that biotechnology will have to offer ought to lead us to reconsider the very way in which we choose to organise our personal lives.[7] This is, I suspect, the proper attitude with which to approach any new technology: neither to embrace nor to reject it impulsively, but to reflect upon what it reveals to us about where and what we are, and what new routes it opens, both for where we might choose to go and what we might choose to become.

Biological parenting weighs us down with responsibility, rendering us possessive and fearful. In our children, it fosters dependency rather than self-sufficiency and serves as a training ground for one-to-oneness in relationships. This itself creates unrealistic expectations leading to a fear of failure and emotional harm that mitigates against the intimacy it claims to foster, resulting in increasing alienation and loneliness.

A broader, non-biological, "networked" family could offer support, security, autonomy and diversity, without compromising in terms of intimacy and a sense of belonging. It is said, "It is a wise father who knows his own child". Presumably it would take an even wiser child to know her own father. But perhaps one day we shall come to believe that the very wise child won't even want to know, because for her, and her ectogenetic society, it won't matter.[8]

Notes

1. Thanks are due to Carole Ulanowsky for her helpful editorial comments on an earlier draft of this paper.

2. By claims of belonging, I do not intend simply the use of possessive

pronouns, for in that respect, the daughter might speak of "my father" as readily as her father would speak of "my daughter". The point is rather that the child (often especially the daughter) is held in this culture (and in many others) to belong to the parent (often especially the father) in a way that renders quite a different sense to the parent's use of the possessive pronoun from that of the child. For the sake of clarity, the slave who speaks of "*my* master" implies a very different sense of belonging (that of being possessed) from the sense implied by the master's use of "*my* slave" (that of possessing). (See also note 3 below).

3. Although we may nowadays be more reluctant than previously to speak in terms of *owning* our children, nevertheless it seems clear that as soon as parental authority is challenged from outside (be the source of challenge the State or private citizens), parents very quickly adopt an attitude of, "What right have you to tell me what to do with my child?" Whilst I do not deny that most parents have the welfare of their children to the front of their minds here, it seems quite clear that the old proprietorial impulse is also at work. The parent sees her/his own rights as being infringed. I am grateful to Alan Milne for raising this issue.

4. None of what I say here is meant to suggest that children are to be treated as fully autonomous beings from the moment of their birth. My purpose is to suggest that adult guidance ought to take the form of temporary "stewardship" as opposed to "dominion".

5. It is worth considering again the Frog joke and asking ourselves where the line is to be drawn between *protecting* children from sexuality and *controlling* their sexuality. (See also Piercy pp.138-139). The unencumbered expression of sexuality is a fundamental element in the transition from dependent ("partial") person to mature adult, and attempts to control this liberating force, be it by parents, the State or society have regularly been cloaked in bogus claims of protection.

6. The film *Shadowlands* presents a neat expression of this danger. Towards the end of the film, the character C.S. Lewis is heard explaining his almost lifelong, debilitating fear of intimacy by reference to the extreme pain of loss caused by the death of his mother. Whilst accepting that this is fiction, it does not seem unreasonable to point out that certain fictional representations have a "ring of truth" to them which warrants careful reflection.

7. It has been suggested that the ideas that I put forward here will carry a hint of menace. Let me therefore be quite clear: when the age of ectogenesis

87

is upon us, I do not foresee pregnant women being dragged, kicking and screaming to the Abortion Camp because biological reproduction has been outlawed. My only intention is to make us think about the options that this technology may offer. The possibility of the responsible use of technology seems to me to require just this kind of anticipatory reflection. Others may come along with argument or evidence which shows the desirability of continuing with biological parenting. However, even if this is so, once we have the capacity for ectogenesis, biological reproduction will never be the same, since it will then be entirely a *matter of choice*.

I am grateful to Lucie Armitt for raising this issue.

8. My aim herein has been to present a critique of the biological, nuclear family unit, couched in terms of the possibilities presented by an alternative system. My criticisms should not be read as aimed at specific "dysfunctional" families, rather I have tried to show that the failings are systemic, not individual.

Bob Brecher (one of the contributors to this volume) has asked what, in my analysis, addresses specifically the *biological* as opposed to the *nuclear family*. It is true that many of my criticisms seem to highlight failings with the latter rather than the former, such that it might be asked, "Wouldn't the return of the extended (biological) family address most if not all of the issues I have raised?" Certainly I suspect that any more supportive arrangement would alleviate some of the problems I have indicated. However, our prejudice towards the biological (as opposed to the simply nuclear) family are so strong that many of us still speak easily of the "real" parents of an adopted child when we mean, of course, the biological parents, and many of the problems of control I speak of are, I suspect, closely linked to the image of my child as being (in a quite literal sense in some parents' minds) "a part of me". For biological mothers in particular, there are clearly grounds for such a claim along what could be termed a labour theory of parental rights. It is only by moving away from this that we can begin to distinguish between the production of goods and the reproduction of persons. The worker (in combination with the work process) creates the commodity in a quite conscious and deliberate manner, a manner which permits accurate prediction of the nature of the end product, since the material being worked on is (generally) passive and inanimate. The nurturing of the child (post-natally) involves the child herself in a very active way as a developing human being. In this situation, the parents are not the creators of the child, as the worker is the creator of the commodity, they are rather (a part of) the environment in which the child, herself, develops. It is this notion of the parent as responsible for the "final product" of the mature human being that I hold to be not merely oppressive for both parent and child, but also as being (possibly inextricably) linked to biological reproduction.

Bibliography

Hearn, J. (1987), *The Gender of Oppression*, Wheatsheaf Books, Brighton.

Piercy, M. (1979), *Woman on the Edge of Time*, The Women's Press, London.

Reiman, J.(1977), "Privacy, Intimacy and Personhood", *Philosophy and Public Affairs*, Vol.6, pp.26-44.

6 The family: Whose construct is it anyway?

Neil Leighton

From the point of view of adults, the experience of the family which they create for their children is a matter of preference. From the point of view of the child it is a thing given or not given; it is the source of the earliest personal experiences outside the womb (or test tube). Since the child, unlike the adult, is not free to choose among alternatives, it would seem that in the evaluation of family patterns, the child's interests and viewpoint must have moral priority over the preferences or opinions of adult contributors to any discussion.

This paper takes as a starting point experience of state provision through local government authorities, the Social Services Departments, in efforts to provide alternative nurturing and upbringing for children whose parents are unable to care adequately for them. The evolution of care systems can be regarded as empirical attempts to offer alternative experiences in the place of biological families. These have been evaluated by the recipients, the children, through their lived reactions -critical narratives of the success or failure of their socialisation. The weighing of the views and interests of such children in the Family Courts is carried out by a Guardian-ad-litem who is appointed by the court to prepare an assessment of the interests of the child in the light of the current circumstances and the history as recounted by different parties. The Guardian's task might be described as attempting to reconcile personal myths and discoverable truths, to identify the interests of different parties and to explore the extent to which they coincide with or conflict with the interests of the child. It would seem that such a task is very similar to that of this present exploration because the concept of *family* is multi-faceted; myth merges with dreams, nightmares and idealisations. But the experience of children of a family might take moral precedence over the politicisation of the

91

concept by adults. This paper will attempt to present children's views and attitudes to family, building upon the experience of children who have been within the state system for, at least, part of their lives. These children have had the opportunity to stand back from their own birth parent experiences and have experienced alternative nurturing patterns in families other than their own and therefore bring an objectivity of viewpoint which is not available to those who have only one personal experience of family.

The state, expressing itself through local authorities in England and Scotland, has an unequivocal duty to provide an upbringing for any child who is without parents. A minimalist model of this activity may be a useful tool for examining alternative nurturing practices.

Input ----------> Care System -------> Output

The input is a child without functioning parents and the required output is a socially competent adult. A care system fails if it does not produce this output. So an ideal care system is one which provides the child with experiences which will give the potential for a child becoming the *best imaginable person*, given the material available to start with. When care systems are chosen or alternatives to traditional birth and nurturing systems are promoted, we cannot avoid looking at what is being regarded as the desirable outcome: the image of what it might be to be human.

It may be possible to get reasonably close to agreement about the *minimal* expectations of socially competent adulthood, but entrapping a consensus vision of possible ways of bringing about human flourishing is a more daunting prospect. It involves as Sartre puts it, a "surpassing" of our own expectations of ourselves, thus a recognition of the extent to which we fall short of what we might be with regard to our own aspirations. (Sartre, 1957. pp. 186-192.)

Logic and language

The language and reasoning which some analysts apply in the field of human behaviour and relationships often do not respect the complexity of the phenomenon: they are reductionist in effect in order to make the material fit the tools that they have available. They do not take to heart even the position of the physical scientist (for example, the phenomenon of light may be recognised as sometimes satisfying the rules of a wave theory model and sometimes the rules of a particle theory model). Human behaviour may similarly be disciplined or directed by rules of reason, but instincts and emotions and perhaps aesthetic considerations may initiate, dictate or influence actions which follow more subtle and ill charted rules than those of reason.

The rules of reason and logic, as popularly understood, assume a single meaning to the words used, a brick is a brick in the sight of all, once defined. One brick and another brick make two bricks but the same is not true of drops of water which do not have fixed boundaries. Like drops of water, personal behaviour, as indeed relationships, do not follow the logic of simple addition. The rules governing our perceptions of the performance of human relationships are inextricably bound up with our views on the nature of being human and assertions about possible future patterns of relationships which must be carefully examined for the presumptions which they embody.

The words used in connection with human relationships linking to a sense of being, such as "family", "sense of belonging" and "awareness of self" may appear to be clearly perceived from outside the relationship. However, closer examination reveals that they are not understood in the same way even by different parties within the relationship, let alone by observers from outside. The English language, when used literally, imposes its own limitations upon our attempts to ensure that we have a common understanding of different perceptions of relationships. Sartre in his attempt to chart the territory in French had to resort to composite words, "l'etre-pour-soi and l'etre-en-soi," the being-for-itself and the being-in-itself, for two forms of consciousness of the self and many more for the different forms of the presentation and appearances of the self in its relationships. The linguistic limitations in Western Europe reflect the lack of attention in both the secular and religious traditions to *interior* lives. Self-examination has been seen as the territory of the mystics and mystical literature even from within the established churches, has tended to be regarded with great caution, judged even as a form of deviance, if not heresy, particularly by the conservative traditions of the Church. It has therefore had little impact on our language. It appears that in the East there are fewer inhibitions, Helena Norbert-Hodge recounts that in the land of the Ladakh, a neighbour to Tibet, the verb "to be" has more than twenty variations depending on the relative intimacy of both the speaker and the listener with the subject matter. (Norbert-Hodge, 1991.)

In the sciences there is a readiness to recognise how the limitations of the available tools or of mathematical techniques restrict the ability to comprehend or accurately describe or measure certain phenomena. Some philosophers have been less cautious than scientists in accepting the limitations of their chosen linguistic tools to comprehensively embrace human behaviour. They have not shown appropriate reserve in venturing into judgement of family situations. A simple example of this is the use of a phrase, when discussing possible future family structures, "The child should be allocated to three adults." This appears to have meaning as an objective statement but implicitly the child subject has become an administrative unit or statistic and the child will reject this conception of itself as a "being-who-maybe-allocated". This might be contrasted with a child who perceives themselves as "one-who-is-chosen", a popular compensatory image offered to children who have been adopted has to come to terms with the earlier experience as "one-who-was-not-wanted" by the birth parents. The notion of "allocation" appears to deny both the child and the adults involved the idea of personal commitment which elsewhere we would regard as of great significance in nurturing. If a child is not an administrative unit like a brick might be, then the statement has little more logical integrity in relation to its subject matter than an instruction to cut a cup of water in half to make two smaller cups - it just does not function that way. If a *self* is to emerge from the process of a nurturing system then the descriptions of the process must reflect the nature of the self to which we must be committed at every stage in the process. It will be suggested later that in relation to bioengineering it may be that the process itself, as well as the account of it, may undermine some of our cherished notions of self.

The best imaginable person

This nature of the self which is the desired output of a care system, or a family, needs detailed description, but what is its form? There is a fable of two ancient tribes living in a desert land where the soil was porous and there was no standing water so that no-one could learn to swim. Occasionally there was heavy rain in the distant mountains and the water swept across the territory and many were drowned. One of the tribes learned to weave plant stems into thick matting and build their huts on these mats and when the water came they floated and many of the people were saved from drowning. Both of these tribes had a folk tale which told of a place where there was deep water and in it lived a creature called a dolphin which was completely at home in water, it was in harmony with it and mastered it without controlling it: it seemed to belong within it and the description of how it moved suggested joy and freedom and recalled to them the best moments of their own lives when they sang and danced and were joyful. The tale also told of the creature's ease of interaction with others and even of occasions when it appeared altruistic. The tribes looked with admiration and envy at the dolphin who lacked their fears and was at complete ease with its environment. If we picture the regions of the tribes as "reason" and "faith", the water life itself, the dolphin would be our "best imaginable person".

The fable is told to avoid becoming entrapped in arguments about ideals of personhood and presumptions about gender. There *are* ideals but it is clearly, at a minimum level, in the interests of society to improve or at least protect its most important features. Thus, primary among the features of society, must be a system for the proper nurturing of children which will produce a new generation of parents who will once again perpetuate a proper system to bring about "best imaginable persons". It is upon this expectation that this paper will build.

The Hon. Justice Thorpe, concerned at the demands upon the Court system to make evaluative judgements about parenting abilities, sought the advice of the Tavistock Clinic about the parental attributes they looked for when assessing parents. This group of professionals pooled their views and the outcome was a blend of personal idealism, points drawn from experiences of care which had failed children and psycho-analytic insights. They furnished the Judge with this list of capacities which they looked for when assessing parents for the family courts. (Thorpe, 1993.)

Their list of attributes could well underpin any alternative care system.

".... Among the capacities to be assessed are:

1. the capacity to anticipate difficulties;
2. the capacity to empathise;
3. the capacity to protect;
4. the capacity to stimulate;
5. the capacity to imagine what it is like to be a child;
6. the capacity to make commitments;
7. the capacity to show love and approval;
8. the capacity to let go and relinquish."

The writers continue. "... While many of these capacities may be *learned*, the basic resource must be there. Our early experiences are fundamental. In parenting we draw upon our own experiences of being parented." (ibid., p. 294)

Is the above list a set of skills which can be taught, learned and practised by imitation by all save those suffering from some personality disorder or pathology? Does it make any difference if, for example, the showing of love and approval is professionalised into satisfying the child's need to *appear* to be loved and approved of?

The features of such a relationship appear to be that it is person-to-person and mutual, that is to say it exists between two people and is believed by each of them to involve the other and to be perceived by the other in the same way as by the self. At the extreme, infants fail to thrive physically as well as emotionally in the absence of that personally directed attention which gives rise to attachment. These same features seem only to have meaning in the context of an awareness of the self and of the other as "persons", experiencing commitment and love, but clearly children are able to experience the sensation of being loved long before they are capable of conceptualizing it. There would seem to be no problem therefore in terms of bringing up very young children, to *simulate* the experience of attachment, the "bad faith" of imitation and falsification of attachment may only be a problem for the *adult* in the arrangement, if there is any problem at all. The offer of a relationship does however require its acceptance by the child whose preparedness for that relationship cannot be taken for granted. It is the child who takes possession of the experience or does not. Older children are very perceptive of the *simulation* of commitment or of its being polluted by financial gain in substitute families.

Personal value

There seems to be some inverted *proprietorial* sense in children that they ought to be loved for their own sake and that they are devalued by any compromise. We, as adults, may feel that it is inappropriate to dedicate too much of our own freedom to our children and in turn that we should not feel possessive towards them. We associate possession with property, but our children may desire to belong to us without compromise. These needs pose problems in the state system where experience has shown that personal nurturing can be most economically and effectively provided by paying foster carers sensible remuneration in a competitive market, for their talents. The carers are of course assessed for their ability to offer appropriate levels of emotional involvement and commitment to the individual child. (This may mean professional detachment where it may be required by an adolescent who has had previous attachments betrayed.) The problem for the children is differentiating between whether they are valued for themselves, (are the subject of a person-to-person commitment), or whether they are valued for the income which their presence generates. (This income may be essential to their carers.) For the child who lacks self-esteem, who has not been used to being valued for their own sake, it is easier to settle for the more cynical of the presumptions as long as the payments continue to be made. Many harbour such scepticism long into their adult lives in spite of continued evidence of commitment after payments have ceased. Interestingly, this phenomenon does not seem to arise for children whose personal care has been purchased by their own, biological parents in the form of nannies or day-minders, where the parent remains in close contact. For these children it seems that the personal involvement from their parent is a pleasant and unexpected bonus to the professional service which is provided. In this case there must be, at some level, consciously or unconsciously, a question in the child's mind, "What is a parent?" when all the tasks of parenting are delegated and, "What do I mean to my parents if they spend no time with me?"

The public care system has not however found a generally more effective model for nurturing than a "family" situation. Options for care include adoptive homes without financial support; adopters receiving allowances (particularly for handicapped children); residential group homes and boarding schools, some of which may have children for 52 weeks of the year.

The child's response

It has been suggested above that whilst patterns of care may be offered to children with the best of intentions from the carer, its acceptability for the child depends upon the child taking possession of what is being offered and making themselves vulnerable to its influence. A child takes an attitude towards their nurture. How does this attitude develop?

"Attitude" is the child's stance in its relationship to the world outside. There is scarcely a matter of choice for the very young infant in relation to the carer or parenting figure because of the situation of total dependency. This is the first context within which the child "learns" or internalises an image of what it means to be loved, to belong, to be valued: this embodies such words as "intimacy" and "affection".

When a child has emerged from the earliest weeks when gratification of basic hungers is all that life is about, it is more difficult to make reliable presumptions about what understanding the child has of the expression of intimacy and affection. From a very early age, the Freudian psycho-analytic presumptions of the dominant influence of sexual drives and appetites intellectually connect intimacy with sexual feelings or thoughts and makes certain presumptions about the source of restraint or censure of the expression of those drives. Children who have been subject to physical violence and/or sexual experiences within their birth family and who have had no other nurturing experiences have no basis for supposing that these activities are not inextricably part of affection and intimacy. They have not the grounds for perceiving those experiences as abuse, as bad and unwanted. Other children's experience of parenting may be less obviously negative but, in some cases, physical contact may be present neither as an expression of abuse or of affection and the child may then have a limited mental picture associated with the experience of affection. Like the word "red" to the colour blind, "affection" may have no meaning or the meaning of it may be profoundly different from common perceptions. It is not however only "affection" and "intimacy" which may be misperceived by children or adults who have not overcome their early life experiences; additionally they may have difficulty with the expression of such concepts such as "family" and "belonging". The danger is that each of the participants in debates on these issues thinks that when a word of this kind is used it means the same thing to the listener as it

97

does to the speaker whereas meaning in this context has both a qualitative and a quantitative component. A relatively trivial example of this may make the point. A solicitor who had read a report relating to a child in the court on a family matter where the writer had indicated the possible negative effects upon the child of being sent to boarding school, said, after the hearing, "I had never thought about it in that way before but I realise that after I went to boarding school, when I was ten, home was simply a place I went to in the holidays and I still have that feeling when I visit my parents now." We can speculate what this experience did to this person's concept of "home" and additionally, it would be useful to ask, what did it do to his concept of "family"?

This account of some aspects of childhood thinking and attitude development is included to illustrate the induction of a personal emotional repertoire or *lived language* of internal experiences. These are constituted from an awareness of certain emotional experiences but can arise also from an awareness of their absence. Arguably, without an experience of love and acceptance there cannot be a proper recognition of its absence from personal life.

The Tavistock list offered a skills list for parenting and included the necessity for deep personal connection between parent and child. The account of the child's development of self-concept that followed illustrated the dependence upon personal emotional experiences *for* that concept. Is that the only material from which our emotional competence is constructed?

Functional relationships

An Irish lady cared for her daughter's illegitimate son from his birth and led him to believe that she was his mother. When he was twelve, at school, the headteacher said to the grandmother, in front of the boy, "Of course you are not Liam's mother are you ?" On hearing this, Liam ran away from home and a social worker went to see his grandmother who was mystified by his behaviour. "Sure I've done everything a mother ought to do for her child so that makes me his mother doesn't it ?" she said. It may be Irish logic but the notion of what might be called a *functional* definition of parenthood is not unfamiliar. The English drafters of the 1989 Children Act had no reservations about ascribing to anyone to whom the court made orders allowing them legal custody of a child, *parental* responsibilities. At the same time the Act withholds from the natural father any legal status. Thus you can be the *father* but not be allowed to assume the role and you might not be the *father* but be assigned the role of *parent*. More obviously, the Irish lady's position is replicated in the Human Fertilisation and Embryology Act (1990) which does not require disclosure to the child that his father is not the husband of his mother; in cases of artificial insemination or in cases where neither of the parents is genetically connected with the child, disclosure of the child's natural origin is not required.

It was clearly not enough for Liam that he had been offered all the experiences of a mother's care, that he had been chosen and loved by his grandmother. He was, after the revelation, no longer the person he thought he was. His grandmother was not the person he thought she was and, above all, the relationship that they had had was not what *he* thought it was. His grandmother could adopt him and that would make her legally his mother, he could then perceive himself as somewhat more her child but he could never, in some sense, *be* her child. The law would, after adoption, describe his birth mother as a "former parent" but in the mind of a child there can be no way in which their biological parent can cease to exist, even if they have no legal rights or responsibilities.

Truth telling

There is a growing body of research which emphasises, for the stability of adopted children, the recognition and acceptance of their birth parents. Arguably, the child who has lost his birth parents or never known them, must be aware of them as a ghostly absence from his life and history. In the birth parent is the beginning of the narrative of our lives. Some would argue that there need be no problem for the child who is not the natural child of his surrogate or pseudo parents or his adopters if he is never told that he has other genetic connections. Is it right to assume that to do everything a parent ought to do for a child makes you his parents? We sensed that the Irish grandmother had somehow missed something when she said this. Pure psychological behaviourism might suggest that if it can be assured that the child's origins are never revealed, then there is no problem of a discrepancy between the identity of birth parents or genetic parents and the identity of the pseudo parents.

The pseudo parent knows that things are not as they seem, that there is an essential falsity about the situation so long as the truth is not shared. This is made more potent in the most common situation of *pseudo-parenting* when it is entered into because of the inability of one or both partners to have natural children. There are two realities which they are reluctant to be reminded of. As we saw with the Irish grandmother, there will be different understandings in the minds of the parents and the child: she knew the truth and lived a lie and he lived life within a false scenario and did not suspect the truth. The emotional transactions between them were never on a shared basis, if there was apparent mutuality it was imbalanced and she was aware of the lack of integrity of her position.

If the truth is not shared, it is hard to imagine that the relationships will be unaffected. People devise psychological tricks to live normal lives whilst harbouring unpleasant memories. For instance, sexual abuse in childhood can be lost to conscious memory or the experience assigned to another personality within the self (but the dismissal of part of oneself or the construction of multiple personalities does not promise a healthy form of development). Does integrity in relationships matter? It can be felt to be a personal affront when someone tells a lie within a relationship of trust. This might guide our judgement about whether people should be encouraged towards, or dissuaded from, placing themselves in a position where they are promoting falsely based trust in them?

Sartre set out at length some of the problems of truthful living which we resolve by acts of bad faith which appears in existential idealism to carry a role similar to that of original sin in Old Testament theology, a regrettable but unavoidable corruption of the ideal of living a correct life. He did not however suggest that bad faith was ever a course which should be deliberately entered into: bad faith is, like sin, something that should not be promoted. Arguably false positions can be justifiably entered into in the desperate search for an identity of some kind for those who have none, or as a step forward for those afflicted with bad self-esteem, but should they be *chosen* for a child by adults? Artificial and undisclosed parenting must be a classical instance of knowingly entering into bad-faith and inherently dishonest parent/child relationships, creating a high risk of trust not surviving through adolescence to adulthood.

When political assertions are made about family and family values in the context of either party politics or gender and familial politics, it often appears as if they arise from a unitary concept existing, continuous and unchanged, over the lifetime of a child. It is however quite obvious that family and parenting perform quite different social and emotional functions for the child over the life span from infancy to adulthood. These relationship forms respond to different needs as illustrated by the different methods of exercising authority as between infancy and adolescence. Generalisations on these matters mislead: descriptions of parental ways of proceeding should be specific and amplified by example or analogy. Perhaps the adult whose intimate sense of family dissolved when he, or she, was sent to boarding school may resist articulating the meaning of family because of the implicit criticism of his parents inherent in the recognition of their failure to be what they might have been for him.

Parenting is a mixture of attitudes, activities and duties but from the child's point of view, the exercising of those attitudes and responsibilities by a pseudo parent is not *real* parenting except when the child accepts it as such. It would seem fair to say that in the West European culture children first consider "family" and "parents" as meaning birth parents and their connections. When other people substitute for those parents they are recognised by the child as grandparents or nannies or foster-carers. The latter may be known to be the natural parents of other children and the children, whilst being "parented" by them, know that they are not "their" parents. Although the Law may have given the carers what it calls "parental responsibilities", it is only when the child feels that they want to enter into a totally committed relationship to displace any previous real or imagined parents that these people may become parents for that child. The child then takes possession of the relationship and "the family" where they live becomes *"my* family". When children are wrestling with these transitions and confusion about origins and loyalties they often do so focusing upon the word "real". "Which is my *real* Dad ?" This is similar to the Irish grandmother example - the functional definition of the parent being the person who parents is not, on its own, enough for the child and the reality of the birth parent is only cast off with reluctance.

It is important to explore in some detail the way children ascribe value to themselves and evaluate the significance of "my family" when trying to assess the implications of bioengineering. Here the possible construction of a family which may deny both the truth of genetic origins and the need for a transition of the child's thinking from attachment to biological parents, to commitment to the pseudo-parent, can deny the importance of a truthful narrative for the child.

Children who have been removed from the care of their birth parents, by intention or accident, and have had some experience of living with them, in some sense *know* them, they exist in their awareness as people of a particular kind. They have characteristics which the children associate with the outside world in the sense of *this* is the way things are. When those children experience placement in another family they are offered an experiential basis for comparison with an opportunity to evaluate both their parents and their foster-carers. They become aware of what might be called the matter and anti-matter of family and of both what their parents are and what they are not, or appear unable or unwilling to be. They will also subject their substitute family to a similar scrutiny concerning what they *are* towards *them* and what they are not. However, it is perhaps important to note that, for children, the ability to detach themselves from the particular experiences may be impaired because the self esteem upon which detachment is founded has its origins within the early experiences. Also if the mother is seen by the child as a rejecting person she may be seen as one who is incapable of love and the child has her blood and genes and therefore may inherit this quality, or is it that the child is an unlovable child? "What does it say about me?" the child wonders, "That my parents display some poor personality characteristics?" There are thus genetic components and psycho-genetic components to cause anxiety, arising from the way parents have failed to be good parents perhaps lacking a wholehearted commitment to them and their interests. "If my parents have failed me, might I not also be prone to failing my children?" The exploration of such possibilities appears to be an important component of the personal narrative, which is the lived experience.

Responses to childlessness

The scenario set out above is essential for the successful transition of a child from birth family to a new family through the child taking possession of membership of the pseudo family. This is the model upon which child care professionals base the current view that, for most children, an *open* adoption, where the birth parents are given acknowledgement by the adopters, is better for the security of the placement than *closed* adoptions where the birth parent is dismissed as a thing of the past. (A "former parent" as the legislation puts it.) This professional view is not however supported unequivocally by some childless persons who wish to create a family for themselves by adoption or by some of the policy makers who take the view that contact with, or even knowledge of their natural origins, is not necessarily helpful to children. There are suggestions in discussion papers relating to amendments to the adoption law that in future, less will be made of uncontested adoptions. This would allow applicants to skate over issues of disclosure to their young progeny. It is also true that courts have rarely been prepared to take issue with adopters who do not wish to explain to the child the significance of their natural origins. The reluctance to confront the reality of adoption at the earliest opportunity has however been partly counterbalanced by the fact that the adopted child only receives a short form of birth certificate and at the age of eighteen has had the right to seek out information about the birth parents, albeit conditional upon some form of counselling. Legislation in relation to bioengineering shows less respect for the value of knowing genetic origins. There is no emphasis upon disclosure and, except in cases of surrogate mothers, no entry on a birth certificate will suggest anything other than the falsehood that the child is the natural child of both the pseudo parents. Thus the myth is to be secured and the truth obscured.

If there is justifiable social concern for the plight of childless couples there would seem to be occasion for moral debate as to whether it would not be preferable to facilitate the placement with them of unwanted or orphaned children, albeit adopted from abroad, as adopted children with known histories and origins which are respected and recorded, rather than opting for technological intervention. Currently adoption procedures are subject to greater and greater restrictions, but the facilitation of bioengineering appears to have gone ahead without due regard to the creation of alien persons separated from the true beginnings of their personal narrative, having false relationships with the significant persons with whom they have an important connection in the world.

This paper has suggested that when looking at alternative procreative and nurturing patterns for children we need to spell out clearly what the desired outcome should be and relate this to the reasonable expectations of children within our contemporary world. These would include the development of a sense of self as a lived narrative blending action and memory; that schemes which disregard the children's experiences deny their right to participate in their own histories and their own futures; that the creation of children who have no identifiable biological origin, no identifiable human beginning to their personal narrative may have a sense of alienation to the world in which they find themselves. The pretence that the bioengineered child is the natural child of the pseudo parents presents an experience of family on unsure ground and undermines the essential attributes of intimate human relationships - those of integrity, trust and openness.

Notes

1 The exploration of this in Britain began with Tresiliotis, J. *In Search of Origins - the experience of adopted people*. (1973) The psychological aspects are explored by Brodzinsky and Schechter in *The Psychology of Adoption* (1990) The reiteration of the importance of access to one's past (in current thinking) occurs in *The Journal Adoption and Fostering* Vol 18 No 2 1994.

2 The uncertainties about the layman's views and those of adopters are reflected in *The Adoption White Paper - Adoption the Future* 3 Nov 1993 HMSO and variation to it in *Placement for Adoption - a Consultation document* April 1994 Dept of Health.

3 See, for example, Martin Thomasson, *A Very Wise Child: Ectogenesis and the Biological Family* - this volume.

Bibliography

Norbert-Hodge, H. (1991), *Ancient Futures, Learning From Ladakh*. Rider London

Sartre, Jean-Paul, (1957), *Being and Nothingness* trans. by Hazel Barnes, Metheun, London

Thorpe, The Hon. Justice, (1993), *The Assessment of Personality*, Family Law, May 1993, Bristol.

The Children Act (1989), HMSO, London

The Adoption Act (1976), HMSO, London as amended by the Children Act Schedules 10 and 15

The Human Fertilisation and Embryology Act (1990), HMSO, London

The Code of Practice Human Fertilisation and Embryology Authority (June 1993), HFEA, London

7 Choosing the family

Sandra E. Marshall

"Children by choice, not chance." This slogan, recently enunciated by a government minister[1], neatly encapsulates a contrast between two ways of construing the relationship between parent and child. The minister was, of course speaking from one of these perspectives and against the other. The perspective from which she spoke might, indeed, be thought to be the one which predominates at the political level and is one in which children are seen as objects of choice. (The term "object" here should not be taken as carrying any particular metaphysical weight.) Closer scrutiny of the slogan suggests, however, that there may well be a slide from the idea that every child should be a "wanted child" to the claim that every child should be "chosen"; part of my discussion will suggest that this elision is a confusion, for it certainly does not follow that a child which is not chosen is not wanted. This should alert us to the fact that the notion of "choice" is under specified in slogans of this kind. My interest in this paper will be to explore the notions of chance and choice in the context of two ethical perspectives which form the backgrounds for differing ways of understanding the parent/child relation, and, inter alia, different conceptions of the family. It should be clear, however, that it is not my purpose to argue that either of these perspectives is the one which we do in fact share, or that we ought to adopt. The point is rather to engage in some conceptual mapping: to understand and track the implications of different ways of seeing matters, particularly in the more immediate context of developments in reproductive technology.[2]

Models and perspectives

The two perspectives which form the background of my discussions I call the contingency and the choice models. These models offer notions of agency and individual responsibility against the background of concepts of luck/contingency on the one hand, and autonomy and control on the other. The account I shall give of these will be broad and highly general, so that there may well be a range of possibilities within each perspective at a more detailed level. My concern is with how far developments in repro-ductive technology might render the contingency perspective less of a possi-bility for us, i.e . how far it might be that we can no longer see things in that way, since the ethical concepts embodied in that perspective might lose meaning for us.

Contingency

Moral philosophers have recently drawn attention to the moral perspective which takes luck/contingency seriously as a central aspect of human lives.[3] From such a perspective human agency is, one might say, shot through with luck/contingency. We are vulnerable to it and see our lives in the light of it. This does not mean that we are not responsible, that we see ourselves *fatalistically*; indeed as Nussbaum puts it, a fundamental question at the moral level is:

> To what extent can we distinguish between what is up to the world and what is up to us, when assessing human life? ... The contingencies that make praise problematic are also ... constitutive of what there is for praising. (Nussbaum, 1986, p. 2).

Within such a perspective, Nussbaum argues, the moral weight rests rather more on the agent's character and response to circumstances than on actions and their outcomes.[4]

One may see the family as part of this external contingency: something into which we are born and within which we must live. The nexus of family relations roots us in our lives but need not be a matter of our determining. I do not mean here that it simply has to be accepted, but rather that rebellion, rejection and acceptance will be seen in a particular way. One thing one might expect however, is that values of fortitude and endurance will be central to such a perspective. Central because from such a perspective we recognise that the world is not necessarily ordered to our wishes. We do not control it and we can have no expectation that things will turn out well. The difference between acquiescence and fortitude needs more detailed discussion than I have space for here. The point for my purposes is that such a discussion cannot go on independently of the ethical perspectives which concern me here. To see a response to the world as acquiescence already says something about the way one understands human agency, it requires a notion of choice which is different from that which underpins the value of fortitude. It suggests that there are alternatives, that a different reaction is possible and makes sense. To approach the world with fortitude is not simply to take what comes but to take what comes in a particular spirit: it is a way of facing contingency, not a giving in to it.

Of course, this is not to suggest that "the family" on this model is necessarily something which is to be seen as having to be *endured*, far from it, it may be something to be celebrated and honoured. One possibility that the model allows, then, is that the child/parent relation be construed as a gift relation. Recent discussions of surrogacy arrangements have made use of this idea (Anderson,1990), my suggestion is that this idea belongs within the contingency perspective. At the very least it resides in the idea that whether one has a child or not is to some extent, perhaps *in the end*, a matter of luck. A thought made vivid by the "gooseberry bush" and "stork" motifs. One might also think here of an expression which is still common in some areas (as a matter of anecdote it is one which I have heard recently and is certainly one which my own mother uses): a woman may say that she "fell pregnant" or "fell for" a child. What is crucial to this expression is that it does not mean simply that the conception was *accidental*. The expression is used in conjunction with the idea of "trying for" a child, so that a woman may say that she "fell for" her child when "trying for" one. One may say that these expressions are ways of conveying something about human agency, not that they are a denial of it, or an abdication of responsibility. And such expressions contrast with quite different ways of talking about the processes of conception and birth, as when someone speaks of "making babies", where this refers not to the recherche laboratory methods of reproductive technology but to the ordinary processes of human reproduction.

Elizabeth Anderson characterises the values embedded in the gift relation as those "which include love, gratitude, and appreciation of others," and which "cannot be bought or obtained through piecemeal calculations of individual advantage" (ibid., p. 84). This may be right but it suggests too rosy a picture. Central to the contingency perspective must be the thought that not everyone who wants a child will get one. Some will have none and some will have more than they hoped for or expected. A child seen as a gift may be a blessing, but such a view also allows that a child may be seen as a curse. Likewise one's family may be a blessing or a curse. The responses which these may call for will be part of the ethical content of the contingency perspective. But it should be clear that the contingency in question, is not simply *nature* as contrasted with *the social*, for aspects of the social world, like the family, involve contingency and chance, just as much as nature or biology. Women who "fall pregnant" are not in the grip of some primitive and mistaken beliefs about the relation between human actions and conception. They know perfectly well what the biological facts of life are. What they express is a particular attitude to or way of seeing those biological facts.

The question now, however, is whether the considerable developments in reproductive technology make this perspective impossible. Whether, the fact that babies can now be *made* and that conception is under our control (hence the idea of birth control) leaves any room for the idea of a child as a "gift" or indeed as a "curse". This latter may in fact be of greater significance than the former for it may be that it will significantly influence our moral responses to cases like that of the James Bulger killing. There is more than one possibility here: one is that the baby who is born is seen as a curse because it was unwanted, but, also, a child may become a curse to its parents just because of the kind of child it turns out to be. This idea means recognising that how a child develops is not entirely up to its parents, that there are limits to what we can do in child rearing. A child who is a curse to its parents may also be a curse to itself and someone to be pitied. One can imagine a response of this kind, though I do not say that the contingency perspective *requires* it, only that it makes room for it.

Choice and control

Developments in reproductive technology can be seen as the natural extension of our desire to control our reproductive lives. As I suggest above it is not for nothing that we speak of "birth control" and "birth control methods". We might think then that these developments fit better with our understanding of ourselves from within the ethical perspective which I dub the "choice" or "control" model. Indeed, we might suppose that the developments themselves, our concern to pursue them in the first place, spring from this perspective itself.

The main focus of this perspective is familiar enough: we view ourselves as autonomous agents, capable of reason, and, most importantly, reflective choice, bearing in mind that "reflective choice" is not simply getting what one wants. We stand in the world, as it were, as choosers. In this sense we are in control of our selves and our world. We need not suppose, however, that we *are* automatically choosers quite independently of our circumstances. Rather, the autonomous, rational chooser is an aspiration: it is what we must become if we are to flourish. That is to say, to flourish is, in part, to be a rational chooser. It is important, therefore, that our circumstances be made as conducive as possible to that end. Part of that environment will consist in values like freedom and the rights bound up with it, however that value is interpreted. Similarly, unless a very radical view is taken, one like Plato's for instance, then the family will be part of that necessary environment. One thing then which one might expect to flow from this is a conception of the family as a structure of rights and an object of choice.

There is choice here in two ways. Firstly, one may choose to become the originator of a family in choosing to become a parent. Increasingly the nature of that choice may broaden as our ability to control the biological processes develop. Secondly, although one cannot choose which family to be born into, one may choose to move out of the family relationship, to abdicate from the network of rights and responsibilities. Indeed, it might seem that a natural development of this would be a legal right for children to divorce their parents and opt for more appropriate ones. (This may be contrasted with the idea of rebellion which the contingency model would involve.) The family then begins to be constructed on the model of a contract, which need not mean at all that it is bereft of love an affection any more than marriage itself is. The point is however, that the central values at play will be those of contract, more binding and certain perhaps than the bonds of affection, less subject to contingency. (Or, one might say that seeing oneself as bound by responsibilities which are what one has chosen in choosing to become a parent is the form which parental love takes.)

It is important to be clear here then that the parent/child relation will be one which is structured by a kind of mutuality, formed through a network of rights and duties. Being a parent is something which is chosen, but what is chosen is a role, one which involves being responsible for others, i.e. for the child. Here difficult questions will arise. The question of how far those responsibilities extend is a vexed one. How far should we or can we hold parents responsible for their children, and what rights do children have? What rights do parents have? Further, we might wonder about the connection between the rights of parents and the rights of other members of the community. As just one illustration of this point consider the claim, currently popular, that a child's education should be a matter of parental choice. Parents, it might be thought ought to have a considerable degree of control over where a child goes to school and what it learns, thus it is the responsibility of governments or local authorities to facilitate that choice. What this might seem to leave out of the account is the interest which other members of the community have in the education of its members. Here there may be conflicts of interest which will need to be resolved.

There is though a deeper issue at stake and one which surfaces in a dramatic way once we begin to consider the developments in reproductive technology. The ethical perspective which I have roughly characterised here gives a central role to rational choice, but as I noted above, this does not mean that everyone is necessarily a rational chooser. This opens up the question of how to characterise "rational choice" here. Given that choosing a child is a matter not just of choosing to give birth but of choosing to enter into a relationship structured by responsibilities and rights, is it clear that this is a choice which everyone is capable of making? It surely is not impossible to imagine that some people who might choose to have child do so in ignorance of the responsibilities they are taking on or are incapable of fulfilling them, through wilfulness or inadequacy. Some people, it might well be argued, are not fit to become parents. In most cases there is no question of such unsuitable people being prevented from becoming parents, for the means necessary to do so seem too intrusive and conflicts with the idea of the family as a private rather than a public institution. Yet we may question how far such a view is sustainable when we reflect upon the way in which the developments in reproductive technology have opened up new ways of bringing about children, ways which require those who provide infertility treatment precisely to make judgements about who is a suitable parent and who is not. Recent public discussions of lesbian parenting and post menopausal maternity bring these issues into sharp focus.

Now although it does not follow, on the choice model, that just because something is a possible object of choice, i.e. in a morally neutral sense it is an option, it is therefore an appropriate object of choice: if we consider lesbian parenting or post menopausal maternity from the choice perspective as I have outlined it, there seems little reason why they should not be proper objects of choice. On the account I have given, the relation between child and parent is informed by a conception of responsibilities and rights; to be a parent then is to fulfil a defined social role. Gender and age need make no difference to an individual's ability to fill that role. The arguments against post menopausal maternity are particularly difficult to be clear about: either the objections have to do with the age of the mother or with the mere fact of being post menopausal. But people vary as to their capabilities and some of the defects of age may surely be offset by other virtues which are themselves a function of age. Greater experience and a better understanding of the world, for example. As to the mere fact of being post menopausal, it is difficult to see how this consideration can rest on anything other than a commitment to an evaluative notion of the "natural", an idea which is notoriously difficult to give any coherent account of.

This latter point brings into focus the way in which the developments in reproductive technology may both influence our concept of what is "natural" and reduce the extent to which a biological connection between parent and child is seen as either necessary or fundamental. In their different ways, of course, all methods of producing children involve biology, but the understanding of the parent/child relation as social is further extended by these technological developments. It has always been possible for parents not to have a biological relation to their children: adoptive parents are parents. The responsibilities that adoptive parents have are no less than those which "natural" parents have. There seems no reason why, if we understand the family relation as primarily a social structure, we should give any special priority to the biological relation at all. Certainly there seems to be no very powerful reason why biological parents should be thought of as "real" parents whilst non-biological parents are not. From this perspective, some of the concerns about the use of foetal ovarian tissue in reproductive research and technology will seem odd. The worry that a child could have a mother who was never born is ill-founded because a) there is no *who*, as it were, who was never born. The idea is incoherent; b) *mother* is the person who cares for the child, who performs the tasks characterised by the family relation understood as a reciprocal structure of rights and duties. Worries about how a child produced by using foetal ovarian tissue will understand its own identity relies on a concept of identity and self which is quite different from the one implied by the perspective I am considering here. From this perspective one's identity is given in that nexus of social relations, of which the family relation is only one.

Becoming an autonomous, rational chooser depends not upon biological origins but upon the social environment in which one learns and grows. A large part of the parental responsibility is to provide the conditions for that growth. Now it might be argued that this level of responsibility is too great, that this conception of the family makes demands upon us which even the most emotionally sturdy might find beyond them. Considerations of this kind will raise again the question of how far we are to see the family simply as a private institution, the object of individual and private choice, and how far we should understand it rather more collectively. This is not an issue which I have much space to address here,[5] but one thing is clear, once the family becomes a collective responsibility it is likely to become a matter for decisions of public policy and that will raise further questions at the level of political theory about the relationship between the individual and the state.[6]

A central claim being made in this paper is that developments in reproductive technology sit more easily with the choice/control model than with the contingency model since we can understand those developments as extending the choices available to us. Whether we then accept that they are appropriate objects of choice is a matter for decision, based on the kinds of value which inform that perspective. But now, given that we can and do control fertility, the failure to do so may look puzzling, and worse it can come to look like a radical moral failure. Once we suppose that having children is a matter of choice, because it is something that we can control, those who have them in less than propitious circumstances may seem to be simply feckless. Consider the frequently documented cases of homeless people living in hostel/hotel accommodation who start families or add to their existing one, thus adding to their already considerable burdens. From the choice perspective it is difficult to see how their actions can be described as anything other than at the very least feckless, for they seem to choose to do something which they ought not to do. Their decision to have a child seems difficult to understand, though frequently the people concerned do not describe the matter in terms of choice at all. Which is not to say that they describe it as an accident either. (Sometimes, of course, there might indeed be an accidental conception, since contraception may not be absolutely reliable.) They may speak of the child "coming along", not necessarily unwanted but not sought either. The dictum that every child must be "chosen" and not a matter of "chance", reflecting the choice model as it does, makes compassion for those I have described difficult. I do not mean by this that people do not feel compassion, rather it is that by making choice central to a conception of human agency we may make the grounds for compassion depend upon a more radical lack of choice than that involved in the cases I am considering. It is easy to see then how we might also come to hold those who have handicapped children responsible too, for the greater our capacity to control such things, through genetic engineering for instance, the less we will be able to see the handicapped child as a contingency and the more it will seem a matter of choice and therefore responsibility. There are comparisons to be made here with the way in which discussions about avoidable disease might go. It may not seem unreasonable to hold smokers responsible for their own ill-health, for instance. This does not mean that help will not be forthcoming but it will be help informed by a different attitude to the recipient from the help given to those whom we judge to have been simply victims of events beyond their control.

None of this is inevitable, let me reiterate: it is not my claim that this perspective, or any other, is the one which we should adopt. It seems more likely that our actual moral attitudes and beliefs are informed by more than one ethical perspective, not always compatible with one another. If we find the implications of the choice perspective alarming, then that is likely to be because we also recognise the force of contingency in our lives. The question is how to fit this into the framework of control which we have developed and continue to develop.

Contingency again

I shall approach the contingency model somewhat obliquely to start with. My aim is to see whether it is possible to get the child as "gift" back into the picture but first I want to raise a point about the kind of control which we may be said to have over fertility and reproduction: the control which comes from reproductive technology. In one sense, of course, we have always had control over reproduction. Once we understood the causal connection between sexual intercourse and conception then the easiest way to avoid the latter is to avoid the former. There are all sorts of reasons why this might not be a good idea on a grand scale, though celibacy, understood as a virtue, can have a significant part in some lives; it can also have part to play in other lives as a matter of pragmatic necessity. Once we move to other means of control, however, the kind of control that an individual has is somewhat different. Celibacy, one might say, is wholly a matter of the will, and although the will is no doubt vulnerable to contingency, in the form of temptation and weakness, nonetheless the control to be exercised is a self-control, i.e. control by and of the self. If we stick with a concern to prevent conception for the moment and consider the means necessary to that end, we may see that although we may indeed choose to adopt these means, and in that sense choose whether or not to conceive, the outcome of that choice is still vulnerable to chance, our control is never absolute, short of sterilisation that is. Still, there is a choice to be made, the choice as to whether to set in motion the events however they turn out, and the crucial thing for the choice model is that we exercise control over our own lives not necessarily through outcomes but by making rational choices. Responsibility resides in the choices we make and the way we make them. A reckless disregard for the possibility of producing children as a result of one's own action is what may be blameworthy, not simply the failure to succeed in an attempt to prevent conception.

If we consider the developments in reproductive technology that are concerned with *infertility* rather than *fertility* the picture is somewhat different. Here the question of what the individual controls and chooses is rather more complex. One might say that the decision to seek treatment belongs with the individual whose problem it is, and this is true just in so far as such treatment is not compulsory. However the choice ends there since the decision as to who gets such treatment, who is suitable, who has the best chance of succeeding rests with others, remembering too that these decisions are not simply medical but social as well. Finally, and most importantly for my purposes, the processes by which conception is achieved sever the link between what the agent does and the successful conception. Success or failure may depend upon techniques like in vitro fertilisation, with eggs perhaps which are not the woman's own: the conception is less a result of what she does but of what others do to her. The point about the developments in reproductive technology is that whilst in one way it does extend our control and enables some people to choose to have a child when without such intervention they have no such choice, at the same time it

113

involves a loss of individual agency and intimacy in the process of producing a child. Reproductive technology introduces a collective dimension into the reproductive process, both at the level of physical process and at the social level: who gets such treatment is a matter of public policy. This is likely to involve a different view of life and birth, not simply as a consequence of the practice but as internal to the practice itself. A process which was once mysterious is no longer so, the very fact that it is something which can be observed and which can go on outside the body makes this so. The processes which can be observed in the laboratory are just those which go in inside the body, there is a continuity here but one which extends our notion of what conception and birth can be. Nothing rules out, in principle, the possibility of a child being produced entirely outside the body, in an artificial uterus; in this case we might imagine birth to be achieved by, for instance, the ceremonial unzipping of the bag. Considerations of this kind are what led to the suggestion that the "gift" model of the child/parent relation was not sustainable, I want to outline a way in which it might be resurrected but in this new context of reproductive technology. Firstly, contingency needs to be put back into the picture, we need to recognise the ultimate fallibility of even our most scientifically sophisticated techniques. Secondly, we need to reconsider the idea of a gift.

The gift: Harrods or Father Christmas?

Understanding a child as a gift involves this: a sense that although the child is wanted, whether or not you have one is not up to you. You may try and conceive, and certainly you will not have child without engaging in sexual intercourse (or some other means of bringing about conception) and in that sense *trying* is essential, but the outcome of that activity is a matter of luck. I say "luck" here rather than just "chance" because luck involves the idea that what comes is welcome, to be lucky in life or love is to get what you want, what you think of as worth having. You are not lucky if what befalls you is what you do not want or do not think of as worth having, though it may still be a matter of chance that you do not get what you want, or that you get what you do not want. The stress here is on the way contingency runs through our lives, to see a child as a gift is to recognise that contingency and to recognise too that success in producing a child is not a matter of desert. What comes to us as a matter of luck is not independent of our human activity but it is ultimately independent of our human will. The question is how far it is possible to retain this idea in the face of technology which does seem to extend the scope of our agency and will because it depends upon an extension of our understanding of how the processes work, and thus our ability to control them. The answer to this question will require a closer account of the idea of a gift, for there is more than one way in which we use this notion. The problem for the contingency model is that it ties the notion too closely to the idea of luck. What we need is a notion of gift which is not thus tied.

Consider first of all one familiar model for the gift - some gifts come unbidden and quite out of the blue. So, the romantic bouquet of flowers arrives from the unknown admirer, but these kinds of gift are rare, and would not constitute the model for the idea of gift under consideration here, rather it would be an analogy for case of immaculate conception. Gifts more often come from those we know, unbidden but as an expression of love, affection or gratitude. Gratitude may also imply desert, as with a retirement gift from a grateful employer, and we can see here how the notion of a gift may become distorted, no longer expressing anything much and becoming simply a matter of form.

Some gifts, however, are not as unbidden as those above and may be more closely tied to our wants, this is a model of gift which I shall call the Father Christmas model. The first point to be made about Father Christmas is that he is both mysterious, in the sense of being unseen, though we know perfectly well how he operates, (with various kinds of fairy assistants and heroic reindeer). We know too that he is susceptible to our requests. We can ask for a particular gift and our wish may be granted, but it may not, we may not get the gifts we ask for, though we will get something. How far the success or failure of our request is dependent upon desert is a matter of variation in the stories we tell. Certainly the threat to a naughty child that Father Christmas will not come if she does not behave might suggest that desert is involved, but the experience of most naughty children is also likely to be that Father Christmas is rather more likely to overlook such naughtiness, or most likely never to have spotted it in the first place. The point about the Father Christmas model is that it allows both for the expectation that wishes will be granted and for the joyful surprise that they are. The idea of the child as a gift on the contingency model is analogous to the Father Christmas model, analogous but not identical. There are clearly differences - the kind of mystery that is involved is obviously different for instance but rough analogies will serve their purpose here.

The Father Christmas model brings into the gift relation the idea that a gift is something that we can ask for, what it does not allow is that there is any control over whether we get what we ask for. This is what is needed if we are to extend the gift notion into the area of reproductive technology. Consider then what I shall call the Harrods List model. It is a common, and to many a welcome innovation, for people getting married to provide a list of those things which they would like to receive as wedding gifts (not perhaps a welcome innovation for the manufacturers of silver fish slices). This list is comparable to the Father Christmas list but goes beyond it since the list will include prices and furthermore be linked to a particular store from which the gifts are to be bought. The list is given to the store and those giving the gift can tell the store which they will give. There is a sense then in which the recipients have chosen their own gifts. This feature might be thought to stretch the notion of a gift beyond its limits and it may indeed be that what we are dealing with here is something at the boundaries of our concepts. Certainly there is room for disagreement here, both at a conceptual and a practical level (for these are, of course, not divorced from one another). Some people may resent being presented with such a list, they may say that it is too calculated, that to be a true gift it must come uniquely from the giver and such resentment might certainly seem justified if the idea of the Harrods list is that gifts not on the list will not be accepted, so that the "gift" is then compelled.[7] A gift list ought not to be just the same as a shopping list.

Supposing, however, that we accept the Harrods list model as a genuine model for a gift relation, does this help to keep the analogy of a gift relation alive in the case of reproduction and the family, particularly in the case of some of the highly developed methods of reproductive technology like in vitro fertilisation and gene manipulation?

I suggest, very briefly, that there are two features which are salient. One is that the Harrods list model brings with it the idea that a gift can be the result of a kind of cooperation between the giver and the receiver, so that the gift does not have to be a surprise or chance. There can in this way be a degree of control over the gift. Thus one might be able to see the child as a gift brought about by the cooperation and activity of the parents and those whose skills and knowledge go into the production, recognising too that the outcome is not absolutely under control even then. But secondly, and this is perhaps a negative feature, the Harrods gift model opens up the possibility of seeing the child as a gift all right, but also the possibility of a child which is the result of a specification, a "designer" child one might say. But that is something which no one ought to want, for that, it might be thought is a corruption of the idea of a gift, whether it is a child one is speaking of or a wedding present. Now it may be that there will be some practices, like selecting a child for particular characteristics like sex, appearance, abilities which bring the whole matter closer to the model of a shopping list in which case clearly seeing a child as a gift will make no sense. This does not constitute, by itself, an objection to those practices; what objections there are will depend upon a quite different set of arguments which would show why one should not see a child as an object of selection, which is not to say that a child cannot be properly seen as an object of choice. My concern has been to explore a little more of the landscape of the latter idea.

Notes

1 Linda Chalker, Minister of State, Overseas Development. BBC Radio 4, Today programme, July 1994.

2 I use "reproductive technology" to include everything from contraceptive devices to the most experimental methods of fertilisation and embryo manipulation.

3 Cf. Nussbaum (1986), Nagel (1979), Williams (1981).

4 For a related discussion cf. Murdoch (1970).

5 For a discussion of parental licensing cf. Lafollette, Hugh (1980), "Licensing Parents" *Philosophy and Public Affairs* , 9.

6 One example of this can already be seen in discussions about the right to fertility treatment based upon a putative right to reproduce. Why we should suppose that there is such a right remains obscure, but arguments in this area demand a fuller account of the difference between choices and wants than I have given here.

7 I am indebted to my colleague R. A. Duff for discussion on this point.

Bibliography

Anderson, E. S. (1990), "Is Women's Labour A Commodity?"
Philosophy and Public Affairs 19.

Lafollette, H. (1980), "Licensing Parents" *Philosophy and Public Affairs* 9

Murdoch, I. (1970), *The Sovereignty of Good*, Routledge, London.

Nussbaum, M. C. (1986), *The Fragility of Goodness* , Cambridge University Press, Cambridge.

Nagel, T. (1979), *Mortal Questions*, Cambridge University Press, Cambridge.

Williams, B. (1981), *Moral Luck*, Cambridge University Press, Cambridge.

Notes

8 Justifying monogamy

Steve Wilkinson

Introduction

Attitudes towards marriage and sexual relationships appear to have changed considerably in the last few decades. More than one in three births now takes place outside marriage, divorce and informal marriage ("cohabitation") are commonplace, and someone who suggested that extramarital sex was intrinsically wrong would certainly be considered an extreme moral conservative.[1] In many respects, though, these changes are only superficial. We still, for the most part, live in a "couple culture", where heterosexual monogamous relationships are regarded as the norm, as desirable and good.[2] The monogamist culture has been reformed, but not overthrown, and what I shall examine in this paper is whether there are any reasons to support the principles underlying it, any reasons to think that it is better to involve oneself in a single, central, relationship rather than a set of non-exclusive ones.

The obvious reply to this is that successful monogamous relationships allow both partners to satisfy desires which they would not otherwise be able to satisfy, including the desire for a stable domestic and/or economic partnership; the desire for one's own children and an appropriate environment in which to raise them; the satisfaction of sexual desires, and the desire for loving, intimate companionship. Monogamy clearly can provide most of these things and this may lead one to think that it is the best, perhaps even the only, way of providing them. What I question in what follows, is whether this is in fact the case. Is monogamy the best way of satisfying our basic wants, or might there be some better way?

First, I shall outline some ways in which one may try to justify monogamy. Second, each of these justifications will be analysed and criticised. Finally, I shall argue that each justification fails and that there are some positive reasons

119

for abandoning the monogamist conception of personal relationships.

Three justification strategies

I want first to outline three reasons why one might advocate the monogamous lifestyle. Undoubtedly, there are others, but the ones discussed are those which (a) have a relatively high level of initial plausibility and (b) are actually advocated by defenders of monogamy. This section provides just a structural sketch of these justification strategies.

Moral objections to sex outside monogamy

The first justification is based on an ethical thesis, on the view that sexual desires can only be satisfied in a morally legitimate way within a long-term, committed relationship. Many orthodox Christians hold this view, believing that sex within monogamy is the only morally acceptable form of sex. Dr George Carey (the Archbishop of Canterbury) has put forward this kind of view, expressing concern over the fact that "gratification" and "sexual and emotional fulfilment" are nowadays often "divorced and decoupled" from "life-long commitment", and claiming that "sexual activity is legitimate and good only when it is an expression of deep, long-term commitment".[3]
    If we support this view, we seem compelled also to support monogamy, or at least something very close to it. If we want our sexual desires to be satisfied and want them to be satisfied in a morally legitimate way, then we shall have to practise monogamy. The alternatives (at least for the vast majority of us) will be unacceptable: these being either abstaining from sex altogether, or knowingly indulging in immoral behaviour (sex without commitment).

Desires which only monogamy can satisfy

The second justification rests on a thesis which could be taken as either conceptual or psychological: that there are some desires which can only be satisfied through monogamy. Clearly, there is a trivial sense in which this is true. There are some desires which are conceptually related to monogamy in such a way that only monogamy can satisfy them: most obviously, the desire for monogamy itself. However, appealing to desires like this will not help the case for monogamy, since they presuppose precisely what is at issue: the desirability of the monogamous lifestyle. So for this justification to get off the ground what is required is for there to be some desires such that:

1. They are commonly, or universally, possessed.
2. They are not merely redescriptions of the desire for monogamy.
3. Monogamy is the only possible way of satisfying them.

Pragmatic justifications

The third type of justification is similar in structure to the second, but rests on an unambiguously empirical thesis: this being that there are some desires which are *most effectively* satisfied by monogamy. This justification is an entirely pragmatic one, which will hinge on factual claims about humanity in general, specific individuals and our particular social environment. It may, therefore, turn out to be the case that monogamy can be justified in this way in some settings but not others.

Moral arguments for sexual exclusivity

Is there any reason to think that sex outside an exclusive relationship is morally wrong? Leaving aside religious grounds for holding such a view, the only plausible arguments are those which attempt to convince us that this kind of sex has harmful consequences of some sort. We can divide the arguments into two categories: those which draw our attention to the immediate dangers of sex outside monogamy, and those which seek to persuade us that sex in general would become devalued, in some way, if we came to regard sex without commitment as permissible.

Arguments in the first category can be largely disregarded, for the simple reason that most of the dangers cited are avoidable. It might be claimed, for example that "casual" intercourse increases one's chances of acquiring (or causing someone else to acquire) a sexually transmitted disease or that it may result in unplanned pregnancy forcing the woman, or couple, to choose between abortion and raising a child in an unsatisfactory environment. Clearly, these dangers are not slight and one ought to take reasonable measures to avoid them. However, this in itself is not sufficient to justify the claim that sex outside monogamy is itself immoral.

The right view to take here is well expressed by Adler (1991, p.127):

> ...simple fornication is not morally wrong, and ... no sexual acts which yield mutual pleasure to consenting individuals can be condemned as perverse or unnatural. But this must not be interpreted to mean that sexual behaviour is subject to no moral restrictions whatsoever. On the contrary, it is subject to the same kind of moral restrictions that are applicable to other forms of playful activity ...

So although participants in sex are subject to a range of moral restrictions of a general nature, "simple fornication" in itself should not be restricted.

To clarify this further, it may be useful to compare sex with other dangerous but pleasurable activities, such as dangerous sports. For example, when someone goes mountaineering it is obvious that certain risks are taken, risks to oneself and to others. These risks, though, are manageable and so arguably the right thing to say about mountaineering is not that it is in itself wrong, but that those who take part in it are responsible for managing and minimising the dangers arising from it. In short, the participants have a duty not to be reckless. Of course, there may be specific mountaineering practices (like mountaineering in adverse weather conditions) which are in themselves unacceptably dangerous and in such cases it will probably be right to condemn the mountaineer for setting out in the first place. But even in these cases, it is not the mere fact that the mountaineer is mountaineering that is condemned, but the fact that in these special circumstances her doing so constitutes recklessness.

The situation of the mountaineer is (in some respects) like that of the participants in "casual" sex. Like mountaineering, sexual intercourse can generate dangers but, as in the mountaineering case, there are some reliable ways of minimising these risks (most obviously, through contraception). It seems right, then, to adopt a similar attitude to both practices. In both cases, participants have a duty not to be reckless, and provided that they carry out this duty, we ought not to condemn them. As in the mountaineering case, there may be certain sexual practices which are so unsafe that practising them itself constitutes recklessness. But the view that all non-monogamous sex falls into this category seems extremely implausible; for if one's standards for what counts as unacceptable danger are this easy to meet, then a ridiculously wide range of everyday activities (like travelling in cars) will be classified as reckless also. It is clear, then, that the immediate dangers associated with sexual activity are not, in themselves, sufficient to justify the claim that sex is "legitimate" only within an exclusive relationship.

I turn now to the second argument. This approach focuses not on the immediate dangers arising from sex outside monogamy, but on the wider consequences of our regarding such sex as permissible. It is an attempt to justify a rule prohibiting sex outside monogamy, by appealing to the negative consequences of our not having such a rule. Barcalow (1994, p.218) outlines one such argument:

> ...the emotional side of sex that makes it such a meaningful and valuable part of human experience - one of the highest expressions of and most potent manifestations of love, respect, affection, and trust - will be lost in favour of sex purely for pleasure and recreation ... if sex

without marriage is not condemned, then the important and valuable link between sex and love will be severed. Sex will become a matter of transitory lust rather than abiding love, degraded to the level of cats copulating in an alley.

The argument can be reconstructed as follows:

1. Sex has a particular meaning (as an expression of love, respect, affection and trust).
2. Its having this meaning depends on the existence of a moral rule which condemns sex outside monogamy; if this rule were abandoned, sex in general would become less meaningful.
3. The meaninglessness of sex is undesirable.
4. We ought, therefore, to both advocate and act in accordance with the rule which condemns sex outside monogamous relationships, in order to prevent sex from becoming meaningless.

Clearly, the premise that is doing most of the work here is 2 and, not surprisingly, it is also the one which is most questionable. For it is not entirely obvious that we should think of sex as depending for its meaning on the existence of a rule prohibiting it outside monogamy.

Two common reasons for thinking this are the following. The first is to argue that sex is valued as a result of its being (mostly) restricted to monogamy. One of the things that makes it valued, on this view, is the fact that it is *reserved for* people who are in a committed, exclusive relationship. Undoubtedly, there is a little truth in this. If sex with total strangers were commonplace, if it were completely casualized, it would probably be seen as less significant than it is at present. So it does seem right to say that our valuing sex is partly dependent on the fact that it's not the sort of thing that we do with *just anybody*.

This point is not, however, sufficient to justify the particular rule permitting only monogamous sex. The most that it establishes is that if we want sex to be valued, then we should restrict it in *some* way. But the question of how exactly it is restricted is left open. One might, for instance, advocate an absurdly restrictive rule, arguing that we should restrict sexual activity to certain days of the year, or that one ought to earn the right to have sex through undergoing some kind of ordeal or test. The logic of the above argument indicates that such restrictive rules would increase the extent to which sex is valued and so these absurdly restrictive rules seem to be at least as well justified as the monogamist's proposal. Alternatively, one might propose a more flexible rule, arguing that the valuing of sexual activity will be retained provided that we don't completely casualize sex, provided that we restrict it (say) to those people who know each other well. So this argument, although perhaps justifying the existence of *some* restriction, will not provide a justification for the specific restriction advocated by the monogamist.

A second reason for supporting the monogamist's view concerns the relationship between what it is that sex *means* and the practice of monogamy. The argument here is not that sex acquires meaning and value just in virtue of its being restricted, but rather that what it is that we mean, what it is that we express, when we have sex is closely tied up with monogamy and the fact that sex is, or ought to be, confined to monogamous relationships. On this view, sex itself is an expression of commitment, an expression of the desire to enter (or continue) a committed, deep and exclusive relationship. It is argued, therefore, that sex can only retain this special meaning if it is confined to monogamy and so, in order to allow it to retain its meaning, we should support a rule discouraging sex outside monogamy.

One might compare sex, here, to promise-making. Promising has a certain meaning and its meaning is dependent on the fact that people usually act in accordance with a rule which says that they should keep their promises. If the rule were abandoned, promising would cease to have any meaning. Similarly with sex. It can be argued that sex has a certain meaning (as an expression of commitment) and its meaning is at least partly dependent on the fact that people accept a rule saying that they ought only to have sex with people to whom they are, to some extent, committed.

Again, there is some truth in the argument. It is right to think that the complete casualization of sex would radically alter its meaning. But the monogamist seems to assume that the only alternative to her preferred meaning is no meaning at all, and this is false. If the moral rule condemning sex outside monogamy were abolished (as, to some extent, it has been in reality) then what we express in sex will change. It may no longer be regarded automatically as an expression of commitment. But this does not mean that it has to lack meaning altogether. It may still mean something; but that something will be something other than the expression of the desire to form (or continue) an exclusive relationship. Indeed, it seems most plausible to think of sex as having virtually no fixed meaning at all: to think instead of its being a medium through which a wide range of different things are expressed, as in a view well-articulated by Dilman (1987, p.91):

> Sex is ... a form of affective body-language in terms of which one makes contact and communicates with the person who rouses one's interest, curiosity, tenderness, or who baits, taunts or challenges one in a special way which needs articulation. But the person who speaks it (sexual body-language) does not always say the same thing, does not always seek the same thing. In that sense sex has no specific

content of its own; it takes on the character of the contact two individuals make, or at least long for and strive after. One could also see it as a form of play. It need not involve any commitment and can bring into play almost any part of the person in his responses to the other.

It seems, then, that the right view of the relationship between sex and meaning is this. The monogamist is right to claim that the existence of a moral rule condemning sex outside committed relationships would furnish sex with a certain meaning, but is wrong to claim that this particular rule is the only way in which sex can be rendered meaningful. Other conventions are available and, whilst these may not give sex the exact meaning that the monogamist wants it to have, they will nevertheless stop it from becoming completely meaningless. The monogamist, then, is effectively holding not just the view that we should stop sex from becoming meaningless, but the more specific view that sex ought to have a particular meaning and that that meaning should be closely connected to monogamy. There may, of course, be some further argument available to support this normative claim about what sex ought to mean. But it has, at least, been established that merely appealing to worries about its becoming meaningless is insufficient to ground an argument for sexual exclusivity.

Desires which only monogamy can satisfy

I shall now examine an argument which endeavours to show that there are desires which only monogamy can satisfy and, therefore, that anyone who possesses such desires will have to choose between monogamy and frustration. What the monogamist needs here is for there to be at least one desire which is (a) commonly (or universally) possessed, (b) not merely a redescription of the desire for monogamy itself, and (c) only satisfiable through monogamy. There are several candidate desires, but for the purposes of this paper I intend to examine just one: the desire for love.

The monogamist argues from the desire for love in the following way. First, it is asserted that all (or most) people want a loving relationship. Second, it is argued that love (meaning here sexual or "romantic" love) is exclusive, in that it is simply impossible to genuinely love more than one person at the same time. Finally, it is concluded that loving relationships must, therefore, be exclusive; and that since exclusivity, in this context, is tantamount to monogamy, the monogamist's case is proven. For anyone who wants a loving relationship (and, arguably, most of us do) monogamy is the only option. If people wish to have their desires for love satisfied, they have no alternative but to seek out a partner with whom they can have a monogamous relationship.

In its strongest form, the claim that love is exclusive is proposed as a conceptual truth, a fact about the meaning of the word "love". For example, Luhmann (1986, p.97) claims that:

> ...one of the most obvious hallmarks of the semantics of love (in contrast to ... friendship) is its *exclusivity*, in that it is generally regarded - and there is broad consensus on this point - that one can only love one person at any one time.

It is asserted that a relationship will not count as loving unless it is *exclusive* and further that this conceptual connection is grounded in our ordinary usage of the word "love". The immediate problem with holding such a view is that it seems to rest on an implausible account of what we actually do mean by "love", even if we restrict its application to what one might call genuine cases of sexual or romantic love. As Soble (1990, p.172) points out, "asserting that love is not exclusive is easy, since human experience bears out the claim immediately". To hold that it is extraordinarily difficult to love two people at the same time is one thing, but it is hopelessly extravagant to claim that such situations are conceptual impossibilities; to claim that there has never been and can never be even one case in which someone has two loves. Such a thesis seems not to be consistent with actual usage of the word "love".

Of course, the monogamist could modify the thesis and maintain instead that an *ideal* love would be exclusive. But this is a normative claim about what love ought to be like and, as such, is not one that can be grounded in a connection with a common understanding of "love" and "exclusivity". Alternatively, the monogamist could weaken the claim that love is exclusive, regarding it not as a necessary truth, but as a contingent generalisation. On this view, non-exclusive love is a conceptual possibility, but genuine love will *tend to be* exclusive, for practical reasons. This is, I admit, more plausible, but will only generate a pragmatic justification of monogamy. The problem with the claim that love is exclusive, then, is that if we take it as a strong conceptual claim grounded in the meaning of the word "love" it seems to be plainly false; but if we take it as an empirical generalisation, then it only generates a pragmatic justification.[4]

Problems arise, too, for the claim that love is something that all (or most) people desire. The first worry is that it seems reasonable to suppose that our concept of love is historically and culturally specific. As Solomon (1992, p.153) claims:

> Love as we know it ... is a historically and culturally determined

126

passion, developed ... as the product of socialization and ideas about sex, marriage, the equality of the sexes, the place of emotion in human life, and the nature and meaning of human life in general.

The reason why the historical specificity of love raises a problem is that it makes it obvious that the desirability of love is open to question. It is at least conceivable that a society could manage perfectly well without our concept of love and without regarding love as an object of desire, so what reason have we for just *assuming* its desirability? Of course, none of this counts against the reality of love and the desire for love. They are social and psychological realities in our culture. But attempting to justify monogamy by an appeal to love is ultimately unsatisfactory, since it is in essence an attempt to justify one questionable feature of our culture (monogamy) by appealing to another feature (love), the desirability of which is equally open to question.

There is also a structural problem involved in this attempt to justify monogamy. If it is claimed that there is a conceptual connection between love and monogamy, then it may be successfully argued that anyone who desires love has a reason to desire monogamy. But there is a price to pay. Given the conceptual closeness of love and monogamy, only those people who are *already* committed to the desirability of monogamy will desire love, since (on this view) successful monogamous relationships and loving relationships are seen as equivalent. In other words, this attempt to justify monogamy collapses into the view that monogamy is justified by the fact that (in wanting love) we already want it. Of course, if we do already want it, then we do (other things being equal) have a reason to practise it. But this clearly does not constitute a satisfactory justification of the practice, since what is at issue is precisely the question of whether monogamous relationships are the sorts of things that we (as rational and/or moral agents) *should* want. The question is not "do we want it?" but "*ought* we to want it?". If, on the other hand, love and monogamy are seen as conceptually independent and there is a looser, contingent relationship between them, then it is unclear why the search for love should necessarily be directed towards monogamy. The only reasons for preferring monogamy, on this latter view, seem to be practical ones.

Pragmatic justifications

This brings us to attempts to provide a pragmatic justification for monogamy. The distinctive feature of the pragmatic justification is that it appeals to empirical claims (for example, psychological and/or sociological theses) some of which will be claims only about our particular socio-historical situation. It accepts that there may be no *a priori* arguments for monogamy. The grounds for preferring it, rather, are instrumental. Monogamy is regarded as a maximally effective way of achieving a certain outcome (be it desire-satisfaction, the promotion of psychological well-being, or whatever). It is accepted that this outcome could, in principle, be generated in a different way and that, if circumstances were different, monogamy might not be maximally effective.

I have two aims here. First, I want to examine and criticize some pragmatic justifications of monogamy. Second, and in so doing, I want to propose some positive reasons why we ought at least to consider rejecting the monogamist's model of interpersonal and sexual relationships, in favour of a more flexible alternative. Not surprisingly, numerous attempts to provide a pragmatic justification of monogamy are available. For the purposes of this paper, though, I shall focus on just two: the "childcare argument" and the "psychological health argument".

The childcare argument

In 1993, John Redwood (Secretary of State for Wales) claimed that:

> One of the biggest social problems of our day is the surge in single-parent families... What is worrying is the trend in some places for young women to have babies with no apparent intention of even trying a marriage or stable relationship with the father of the child.[5]

Leaving aside concerns about social security expenditure, the main reasons for finding this "worrying" are likely to be (a) the view that single-parent families provide a relatively poor environment in which to raise children, and (b) the view that the "traditional" two-parent family is an ideal child-raising situation.

These views underpin the childcare argument for monogamy. First, the monogamist asserts that (all other things being equal) two-parent families are preferable. This is usually cashed out in terms of effects on children (it is sometimes claimed, for example, that children from two-parent families are more likely to be happy and less likely to be criminal), but may also take into account the interests of parents. Second, it is argued (plausibly) that parents are responsible for providing an appropriate home environment for their children. Finally, it is concluded that, given this, one should (where possible) have children only within a monogamous relationship and that, having had children, parents should strive to make their monogamous relationships work, in order to sustain a stable home environment.

There are two obvious problems with this. First, it only provides a limited justification for monogamy, since it only applies to people who have, or are intending to have children. Of course, most people do fall into these categories for some part of their lives. But it is also true that most people spend at least half of their lives outside these categories (before and after having raised their children).[6] A more serious problem is that the argument relies on a questionable empirical premise: that "traditional" two-parent families produce "better" children than other arrangements. Clearly, there is not time, within this paper, to fully discuss what is a complex sociological question. I will, however, make just two tentative suggestions.

The first is to point out that there is, as yet, no convincing evidence to support the empirical assumptions lying behind the childcare argument. Even if single-parent families and (say) crime are correlated, it is still far from obvious that family structure itself is the *cause* of criminality. The second is that what is of *fundamental* importance, as far as childcare is concerned, is not the structure of the family, but the quality of the care that is provided. Of course, it is reasonable to think of structure and quality as related; some structures may make it harder for the carers to provide high-quality care than others. But in this respect, family structure is just one of many contributory factors such as socio-economic position, housing, education and the character of the parent(s). My suggestion, then, is that, when considering childcare, we ought to regard family structure as of only secondary importance. Quality childcare can, at least in principle, be provided by a wide range of different family structures and the existence of monogamous parents is neither necessary nor sufficient.

The childcare argument for monogamy, then, is unconvincing for the following reasons. First, it is limited in scope in that it applies only to people with children. Second, its empirical assumptions are, at best, questionable. Third, it seems to overestimate the importance of family structure, failing to see it as merely one of many contributory factors in the provision of quality care.

The psychological health argument

The psychological health argument is based on the thought that one's self-concept, or sense of identity, is built around the close personal relationships that one has. Brenda Almond (1991, p.66), for example, endorses this, claiming that:

> ...a person's sense of self is built to a very considerable extent, possibly entirely, on that person's sense of others in relation. Divested of any intensity of care for close others, a person's sense of self-hood diminishes, perhaps vanishing entirely, until the will to continue in

existence expires.

If we believe this (and it is plausible) it seems wise to engage in caring relationships of some sort, for the sake of our own psychological well-being, if for no other reason. But why should this lead us towards monogamy in particular? The monogamist's likely answer here is that a single, long-term relationship enables one to have an especially stable and coherent self-concept and this, in turn, generates a high level of psychological health and happiness. This is contrasted with the situation in which one is engaged in a number of different intense relationships, which supposedly has the opposite effect: unhealthiness and unhappiness. Soble while not endorsing it, gives us a good description of this argument: (op. cit., p. 176)

> The nonexclusive lover winds up having two self-concepts, and that state of affairs is psychologically stressful and too difficult to withstand on a continuing basis. The nonexclusive lover is courting existential disaster; she is not sure of who and what she is, since she is at once so many things.

The monogamist's conclusion, then, is that if we want a stable, coherent self-concept (and, presumably, we all do) we ought at least to try to form a long-term exclusive relationship.

There are a number of objections to this. First, Soble, (1990, p. 177) rightly points out that:

> Prior to x's loving y, x had attachments to parents, co-workers, and friends, all of whom contributed to x's self-concept. Before x loves y, then, x will already have multiple self-concepts; this is simply a fact of life and not normally an existential disaster.

Soble effectively says that the monogamist is exaggerating the extent to which having multiple emotional attachments causes one to have "multiple self-concepts". Plenty of people are simply unable to have a central relationship and it would surely be wrong to maintain that they all have a serious psychological problem. However, the monogamist could, understandably, argue that what we are dealing with here are multiple *sexual* relationships, not just emotional attachments in general; and that the existence of multiple sexual relationships is a much more serious matter than (say) having friendly relations with a wide range of colleagues.

A more serious objection would be to question the assumption that having multiple self-concepts is a bad thing. One may prefer, for instance, not to see multiple sexual relationships as generating multiple personalities, but rather to see them as addressing the needs of different aspects of the same personality. This well expressed by Gregory (1991, p.91):

> ...if we accept that there are many facets to each personality, then it must seem appropriate that a person should seek out a number of close friends, of both sexes, whose various strengths and sensibilities accord with the diverse aspects of his or her personality. Too great an attachment to a single relationship must normally involve the neglect of some and maybe of many of these facets.

We are faced, then, with a choice between two psychological theses. The first emphasises the dangers involved in having an incoherent and fragmented self-concept, suggesting that multiple sexual relations increase these dangers. The second emphasises the dangers involved in neglecting certain aspects of one's multi-faceted personality: if we base our sense of identity too closely on one central relationship we will ignore, and probably damage, important parts of our self. The real situation, I suspect, is that there is some truth in each view. It *does* seem right to think that someone who tried to involve themselves in a very large number of emotionally intense relationships would be endangering the coherence of their personality. But it also seems right to say that if one is too committed to a single relationship, one is in danger of screening out important aspects of one's personality. So what conclusions can we draw?

First, we can conclude that the "psychological health argument" for monogamy is unsuccessful. To say that it is psychologically unhealthy to have an *excessively* diverse socio-emotional life is plausible, but to conclude that we ought, therefore, to restrict ourselves to just one partner seems unduly extreme.[7] Second, it seems that the considerations discussed above point us towards the stronger conclusion monogamy may, in fact, be psychological unhealthy in some respects.

Conclusions and positive proposals

The arguments in this paper have been mostly negative, in that they have aimed to show that the extant justifications of monogamy are unsuccessful. I wish to conclude, then, with some rather more positive remarks, summarizing the positive thesis that emerges.

What I do not claim is that all monogamy is bad or that we should all try to avoid it, for there clearly are monogamous relationships which benefit all concerned. What should be criticised, though, is the view (prevalent in our culture) that the monogamous relationship is a model around which we should all seek to build our socio-emotional and sexual lives. There are three reasons for this. First, (as I have tried to show) there are no good arguments for adopting this particular model. Second, it seems that there are reasons for thinking that there should not be any such model, in order to allow maximum flexibility and diversity.[8] Third, there are some specific reasons (listed below) for regarding monogamy as undesirable.[9]

1. Many people have a need for socio-emotional diversity and for acceptance by a wide variety of others. These things are liable to be stifled by the existence of a long-term exclusive relationship.
2. Given the multi-faceted nature of many personalities, it seems unrealistic to suppose that most of us will be fully satisfied by just one central relationship. Within the confines of a monogamous relationship, there is a danger that certain aspects of each personality will be ignored and damaged.
3. The expectations generated by our "couple culture" are sometimes unrealistically high. People frequently expect too much from individual relationships and this may lead to the complete breakdown of what could have, in other circumstances, been a valuable friendship.
4. Abandoning the restrictive conventions surrounding sex may have a number of social advantages. For example, Comfort (1974, p.52) suggests that "social sex" may come "to express and cement the equivalent of kinship through a general intimacy and nondefensiveness, reinforced by the very strong reward of realizing suppressed need for variety and for acceptance".

I do not claim that we should aim for the complete abolition of marriage and monogamy, but (given the considerations discussed above) it does seem that we should, at least, be open-minded about the structure of personal relationships.

Notes

1. See, for example, *The Independent* newspaper (27/01/94).

2. The expression "couple culture" is borrowed from Almond (1991).

3. Remarks quoted in *The Guardian* newspaper (04/11/93).

4. Some persuasive arguments against this empirical generalization can be found in Gregory (1991) and Gregory (1995).

132

5. Remarks quoted in *The Independent* newspaper (20/11/93).

6. This point is well articulated in Gregory, this volume, (1995)

7. Socio-emotional diversity and sexual diversity are, of course, distinct and this line of argument is only relevant in cases where the two are in fact connected.

8. There is not space within this paper to elaborate on these reasons. Those that I have in mind, though, are not unlike the thoughts offered by Mill:

> As it is useful that while mankind are imperfect there should be different opinions, so it is that there should be different experiments in living; that free scope should be given to varieties of character, short of injury to others; and that the worth of different modes of life should be proved practically, when any one thinks fit to try them. (Mill, 1962 p. 185)

9. For a much more detailed discussion of these reasons see Gregory (1991) and Gregory (1995).

Bibliography

Adler, M.J. (1991), *Desires: right and wrong*, Macmillan, New York.

Almond, B. (1991), "Human Bonds", in Almond, B. and Hill, D. (eds.), *Applied Philosophy*, Routledge, London.

Barcalow, E. (1994), *Moral Philosophy*, International Thomson Publishing, Belmont.

Brown, R. (1987), *Analyzing Love*, Cambridge University Press, Cambridge.

Comfort, A. (1974), "Sexuality in a Zero-Growth Society", in Smith, J.R. and Smith, L.G. (eds.), *Beyond Monogamy*, John Hopkins University Press, Baltimore and London.

Dilman, I. (1987), *Love and Human Separateness*, Basil Blackwell, Oxford.

Gregory (1991), "Against Couples", in Almond, B. and Hill, D. (eds.), *Applied Philosophy*, Routledge, London.

Gregory (1995) "Why marriage must fail" in Ulanowsky, C. E. (ed.), *The Family in the Age of Biotechnology*, Avebury, Aldershot.

Luhmann, N. (1986), *Love as Passion*, Harvard University Press, Cambridge.

Mill (1962), "On Liberty", in Warnock, M. (ed.), *John Stuart Mill: Utilitarianism*, Collins, Glasgow.

Soble, A. (1990), *The Structure of Love*, Yale University Press, New York.

Solomon, R.C. (1992), *Entertaining Ideas*, Prometheus, New York.

9 Why marriage must fail

Paul Gregory

The claim is that marriage necessarily fails much of the time to adequately integrate our emotional and sexual lives. The failure is of a system of values, not of individuals. Many both outside and within marriage are harmed. This thesis is perfectly compatible with some marriages succeeding and with many succeeding some of the time.

The argument focuses on the rule of fidelity (or, rather, the rule of sexual exclusivity) and the ideal of a single central relationship.

Changed circumstances

Monogamy as an ideal, and especially as the established setting for all sexual relationships, displays serious deficiencies. These deficiencies make themselves felt in numerous social problems and in commonplace unhappiness. Yet it is mostly individuals who are held to blame. Well-rounded persons are blamed for failing to fit into the square hole of marriage.

So it comes about that the estranged parents, the lonely divorcee, the frustrated bachelor, the unfaithful husband, the prostitute and her clients are all subject to the slur of moral and personal inadequacy or, at best, in the latter cases are held to be the semi-willing victims of oppression by the opposite sex.

The opinion leaders of our society appeal for a return to traditional values. But if we have moved away from certain traditional values it is because circumstances and expectations have changed and because, even in their heyday, those values were often contradictory or bogus.

Before examining the concept of marriage as such and the values it assumes, let me state some assumptions and clear the ground of certain related issues which are only sometimes relevant.

Our times have seen sweeping changes in the material circumstances governing our sexual and affective lives. These are:

* Control over fertility. Connected with this is the desirability (in the light of high population levels and high per capita consumption of natural resources) of a low birth rate, and the fact that provision for old age need no longer take the form of having children.

* Acceptance of the principle and partial realisation of substantial equality between the sexes. Connected with this is the material feasibility of single-person households.

These changes (i.e. the attenuation of certain constraints) mean that age-old structures and assumptions no longer hold. While a traditionalist might see in the system of marriage the wisdom of the ages, we have meantime entered veritably a new age.

Definition of marriage

In line with usage in the Western world, marriage here means monogamous marriage and applies also to marriage-like arrangements, e.g. common-law marriages. Much of the analysis also applies to "relationships" as the term is commonly understood.

The principal elements involved in marriage — its defining characteristics — are as follows:

* An exclusive relationship of a sexual nature.
* A single focal relationship, overriding other claims of friendship. The marriage partner is the most important person in the life of the other, both day-to-day and long-term.
* Co-habitation. Married people share a household.
* The intention of permanence.
* Solidarity - notably in times of hardship, sickness and in old age.

The important non-essential element is joint upbringing of children issuing from the marriage. First some comments on this last aspect.

Marriage and parenthood

In appropriate material circumstances, there is no compelling reason why the responsibilities of parenthood must be exercised within marriage, i.e. in a joint household and with a continuing, sexually and emotionally intimate relationship between the parents. All that is required, in practical terms, is that the two households be located conveniently close to each other and that the parents should have a friendly working relationship. (The key material circumstances involved here are flexible working hours or else material independence and, crucially, the availability of suitable housing. It is incidentally apparent that, as a society, we have come to place more emphasis on providing a variety of other goods and services, including many that are doubtless trivial, rather than designing our living and working environments to be adaptive to the lives of the affections.)

It is important to stress that other considerations apply when material circumstances fall short of what is required. Children need stable relationships with adults of both sexes, and the primary obligation to provide those relationships rests with the child's mother and father, often overriding their other duties. (This does not mean that the two child-parent relationships are enough: children need a multiplicity of relationships with adults of both sexes, both in order to correct for the idiosyncrasies of their parents and to provide substitutes in the event of tragic separation.)

Even if the above principle is not accepted (i.e. that parenthood can be adequately provided while the parents retain separate households), there is the further point that, in an average life span of some seventy years, of which over fifty are spent in adulthood, care for children should not *normally* be taking up more than, say, twenty years. There is no reason why the life style for the other half of adult life should be dictated by considerations appropriate, if at all, only to this special twenty-year period. (Following the population explosion and in the light of the high per capita demands currently made on natural resources, it cannot be held "responsible" for more than a handful of people to have more than two children. How you space them is, granted, another matter.)

Practical arguments for sexual fidelity

Traditionally the social and economic need for fathers to take their share of responsibility for any children produced by a sexual relationship has justified a rule of sexual fidelity. But note that this justification was even then only watertight as long as the nature of the sexual intimacy was liable to actually produce children. Today we have considerable control of fertility, with the result that this argument, while retaining some force, is much diminished.

AIDS: In the meantime we have, again, as in some previous centuries, a fatal, sexually transmitted disease. This is a powerful argument for hygiene. It is only a weak argument for fidelity.

In this connection, there is a general question of how risks associated with infectious diseases should be handled. Always avoided at all costs? This would seem to be too extreme. There are sometimes good reasons for taking small risks.[1] Furthermore, we might bear in mind the way we, as individuals and as a (world) society, handle other risks. It needs also to be said that, although the risk may now be nearly everywhere, it is not remotely everywhere equal.[2]

Personal expectations and demands

There have been major changes in what is expected of a relationship. Since marriage is no longer an economic necessity, the focus has shifted from material considerations to personal qualities. A good husband, a good wife, are no longer defined in terms of the fulfilment of specific roles such as being a reliable provider or an efficient housekeeper. What most of us now expect from a prospective partner is defined largely in terms of emotions and personalities, and is hence highly individualistic. Often it is even in terms of shared leisure interests. Typically, enormously complex demands are now made of a prospective marriage partner. It would be too easy simply to censure people for making these demands. If one takes the notion of marriage as a life-long (and sexually exclusive) union at all seriously, then it would seem to be rather important to set higher criteria than those for a simple friendship.

The rationale of fidelity

If monogamy is claimed as the only justifiable setting for sexual intimacy, there must be a rationale for this. At a general level, it can be agreed that humans and human societies have a continuing need (i.e. independent of considerations related to fertility) to integrate sexual behaviour into the life of the emotions. That is, we try to make sexual intimacy expressive of the mutual emotions felt by those involved. More precisely, we say that those emotions should be ones of affection, fondness, liking or love. So far, so good.

The problem arises because of the exclusive nature of the claims, and most notably the sexual claims, inherent in marriage. Presumably the justification for this exclusivity is that the marriage relationship is (ideally) the central relationship in a person's life, with a much more intense helping of affection and love than is to be found in any other (sexually attractive and socially tolerated) relationships. Sexual intimacy is then seen as expressive of the uniqueness of the relationship; extra-marital sexual relationships are ruled as undesirable because they belie or undermine the centrality of the marriage relationship (legitimate sexual intimacy being interpreted as *always* expressive of central emotions).

One assumption here is that a person needs (and therefore should ideally live within) a single central relationship. But it is difficult to see what an argument for this claim would look like. It might be an empirical claim about what people naturally prefer when they are free to choose, but this is a highly theoretical circumstance. Apart from the commonplace that people never grow up within a vacuum, there is the consideration that individuals do not usually have anything like a practical choice in the matter, any more than they have a choice about whether or not to enter a contract of employment of some kind.

Perhaps the argument for monogamy draws its strength from a claim about what kind of arrangement generates the most potential for happiness, fulfilment and the like. Here it would be easy to provide apparent counter-examples. But the claim is too vast for anecdotal matter to decide the issue. Each of us may form a conviction one way or the other; in the final analysis, it seems more like a matter of faith than one for demonstration.

Assuming that sexual intimacy is, ideally, expressive of love, it needs to be demonstrated that it is only possible to love a single person at any one time.[3] This is counter-intuitive. It might, however, be possible to redefine love in a strong sense such that intense love is always focussed on only one person. We might genuinely wonder, for instance, whether it is possible to *fall in love*, or *be in love*, with more than one person at a time. But we might equally question whether such a peak of intensity of feeling can be maintained for long, let alone over a lifetime. If it is not maintained, then there is a justification for either later terminating the sexual intimacy involved in the relationship, or else extending sexual intimacy to a new love.

For the present defence of fidelity to hold, the love ideally present or strived for in marriage has, we have seen, to be either exclusive by definition or else must be a love of such intensity that it practically rules out comparable depth of feeling towards anyone else. Now there is no reason to suppose that life will necessarily present us with a person whom we feel bound to quite this closely and who also, felicitously, returns the feeling in equal measure. It will happen in some lives, fail to materialise in others, and in yet others there will be an essentially one-way affection, at least of this intensity. The move now open to the defence of fidelity is to claim that the special love involved is something which has to be worked at, that it is not a love which just happens.

Now arguably no love just happens; the new affection is tended with hopes and meetings until it is sometimes suddenly - happily or tragically - out of control. But neither can love, as commonly understood, be forced. Yet for his argument to hold, the advocate of fidelity has to redefine love as something that can substantially be controlled, i.e. subjected to the will of the individual. This redefinition is implausible. The common word love involves necessarily a strong affective element and hence a certain spontaneity: love is not invested like trust in a business partnership.

The advocate of fidelity must now move the focus to the marriage relationship as such. The relationship, rather than the sense of love, must be nurtured until, with the years, it has become something special or irreplaceable, i.e. until each partner has become the most important person in the life of the other. "For better or worse," I should sceptically add, for familiarity is not the same as love.

This is the nub of the problem. The advocate of fidelity is eventually forced to discard the centrality of love, at least in any ordinary sense, and replace it with some such notion as long-term commitment. But this makes the connection of the relationship specifically with sexual intimacy ever more tenuous and artificial. The truth of the contention becomes clearer and clearer: the relationship becomes special because it has been made the unique arena for sexual intimacy, while the justification for restricting sexual intimacy to this one relationship is that it is special. That is, a wholly vacuous specialness is manufactured. In other words, there is in principle also no moral reason (there may still be prudential ones) for restricting sexual intimacy to a single relationship.

Mismatches: the non-universalisability of the marriage ideal

In the long term, sexual desires can rarely be ignored with impunity. The following argument therefore assumes that the majority of people *need* sexual fulfilment of some kind and that it is *desirable* that they should find some sexual fulfilment. The corollary is that celibacy imposed by force of circumstance is an evil.

In the last section the point was made that not everyone is likely to meet the person whom they can relate to and love unreservedly and who also, felicitously, returns the sentiment. It was argued that this fact would force the advocate of fidelity to redefine love so radically as to lead eventually to the collapse of his argument.

Now in forming and developing relationships a great deal always turns on just how much compatibility and closeness is demanded. This said, the advocate of sexual exclusivity needs, for his argument to carry any conviction, rather a high level of compatibility and closeness. However, once expectations and demands begin to rise only a little, people encounter difficulty in finding the suitable partner or else they seem to find themselves with the wrong partner. Where does the fault lie, in the people who ask too much, or in the value system that calls for such a high investment in a single relationship?

If the justification for sexual exclusivity is sought in the specialness of the relationship (or else in the specialness of the other person), then we must ask whether everyone can realistically have such a relationship if they so choose. Is this statistically feasible? It would certainly be conceivable for nearly everyone to be a partner in an exclusive relationship of sorts. And equally conceivable for this relationship to be a sexually intimate one excluding third parties. But such partnerships cannot reasonably be expected also to be ones of a meeting of minds, of wide-ranging compatibility, of depth of companionship. Yet once these qualities are absent, again, the moral rationale for fidelity collapses.

The point is crucial, and I will restate it - twice. Assuming affections may be coaxed but not manufactured, and since affections are not automatically mutual or automatically associated with sexual attraction, it is statistically probable that many people will be unmatched or ill-matched. If they are ill-matched, a mockery is made of the whole rationale of sexual intimacy being expressive of the special closeness of the marriage relationship. There is no longer anything inherently unique or especially valuable about the relationship, only the uniqueness imposed externally by the norm of exclusivity in sexual relationships. The justification for keeping the sexual relationship exclusive has to be that the relationship is *on other grounds and in other respects* unique and special such that sexual intimacy and exclusion can reflect this unique and special character. But now, in practice, the only thing special and unique about many of the relationships is that they involve sexual intimacy.

This problem only arises as long as the rule of sexual fidelity, as a moral (rather than hygienic or progenitory) rule, is propagated as binding on all. The ideal of exclusive love (in an ordinary and substantial sense of the word love) as the only proper setting for sexual intimacy cannot realistically be universalised. This does not mean that it cannot be realised some of the time. (It could theoretically be universal in a world which were governed by divine providence and guardian angels, but it cannot be universal in a world subject to the disorderliness of non-mutual and conflicting attractions.)

Here the second restatement of this crucial point, this time in statistical terms. Imagine a model of people forming couples. Let us suppose that the average woman in the realm is three inches shorter than the average man. Let the tyrant decree that each woman is to marry a man who is three inches shorter. We intuitively see that havoc would result, at least in the absence of centralised matching by computer. Our intuitive insight could doubtless be demonstrated by mathematical modelling using probability theory.

Let us now add just one more variable. Suppose the average woman is three years older than the average man and that the tyrant issues additionally a decree that each woman must marry a man three years her junior. With just two variables, the chaos is complete. Yet in the area of personal relationships we are dealing with a multitude of variables.

The ideal and the good

Let us suppose for a moment that a close, lifetime relationship, which is the ideal of marriage, really is a most desirable destiny for all.

(This is a big supposition. The institution of marriage lends legitimacy to the staking of exclusive claims, and hence to possessiveness and jealousy. The latter can scarcely count as virtues.)

Let us suppose furthermore that, notwithstanding the foregoing argument, it could reasonably be achieved by everyone, i.e. that there were no systemic problems about its universalisability. This ethic still runs foul of another difficulty, namely that setting something up as an ideal to be pursued by all is likely to encourage falseness in one shape or another. For example, assuming that sexuality constitutes a powerful drive, if it is only acceptable to exercise that drive in the presence of certain rather high-flown emotions and attitudes, people will consciously or unconsciously fabricate the appropriate feelings. Those feelings, even if they are not wholly counterfeit, will consequently lack staying power.

In other words, once an ideal is firmly in place, people will feel constrained to comply, and be it at the cost of suppressing (either publicly or psychologically) what they really feel and want. In the present case, if it is put around that people (and notably adolescents) can only have sex when what they feel for each other is love (rather than, say, simply affection), then they will either pretend to such feelings or else — and I suspect this is far worse and widespread than straightforward deceit — they will manufacture the said feelings. In consequence, they are likely to confuse sexual desire and love.

Now it might seem that this blending of the two (desire and love) is the ideal state, indeed just what we have been striving for, and in a sense it is. But do we achieve the real thing by censuring (and censoring) the distinction? Or do we not rather thereby introduce confusion into the hearts of the best, while fostering hypocrisy in the rest? The word love is easily spoken, and it is only

142

a little more difficult to imagine that it has been achieved, especially if you have the incentive of socially sanctioned sex to reward you.

The general fallacy at work here might be described as the *confusion of the ideal with the good*.

There is a crucial difference between on the one hand a statement of the form that sexual intimacy *can* be expressive of love (and when it is so expressive this fortuitous event is to be welcomed), and on the other hand the setting up of an ideal unity between desire and love, which all should strive for. There is a presumption here even that we have the power to choose to achieve this harmony. This presumption is, I contend, a form of hubris. Or, in a more modern, a Wittgensteinian idiom, it is what happens when thought is idling. Ideals are the product of idle minds. What we should instead require, of ourselves and of others, is behaviour that is *good enough*.

Summary

First the argument from common experience tells us how difficult it is to find and win someone with whom we can forge more than a limited partnership. Should we then lower our sights? But if it does not much matter whom you marry as long as a rough and ready compatibility is ensured, then equally it ceases to matter that you should be faithful. Unless the argument for sexual exclusiveness is to be one of fidelity for its own sake.

The empirical premise of this argument, namely the practical difficulty people face when seeking a suitable partner, was then shown to be a nearly necessary truth. That is, the statistical probability of no or few placement difficulties arising is negligible. Hence, the failure of marriage as a social system is pre-programmed, and does not generally reflect personal failings. (This argument from non-universalisability does not presuppose acceptance of a Kantian standpoint, although a Kantian would have to accept it.)

Finally, a separate argument distinguished between a set of circumstances being good in the sense of felicitous and these circumstances being an appropriate target for acts of will. We should not seek to control and determine everything, because the attempt is likely to fail and, indeed, create more havoc than letting things be. In matters connected with sexuality, it is arguably wholly inappropriate, for spontaneity is of the essence here, the nature of the erotic experience being a letting go, an abandon, and so a relinquishment of control.[4]

Notes

1. If sexual intimacy really can be the insistent expression of love, and is sometimes at least not indulgence, then it can equally sometimes have an imperative place within a relationship. In a specific case, the risk to be avoided may really be negligible, and, on occasion, a premium might rightly be placed on the wholesomeness of the intimacy. When there is talk of risk, most people in most circumstances will think first of that of an unwanted pregnancy. There is a matter of values at stake here, and the choice need not always fall in favour of restraint. Living a life, like giving life, involves taking risks. This does not mean that risks should be taken often or blindly.

One thesis of this essay is that it is natural and right for people to want some sexual variety, ideally in order to reflect and express something of the scope of their affections. Because the fidelity mandated by monogamy is so absolute, people give way to "temptation", and when they do so they may well enter risks which are indeed ill-advised. The scenario I am advocating, on the other hand, involves licensing some sexual variety, namely within a very few long-term alternative relationships, with the result that the desire to indulge in ill-advised adventures is much abated. Having two or three or four long-term friendships with (an occasional) sexual component (i.e. among other components) is not promiscuity; on the contrary, it is monogamy that gives rise to promiscuity because much of the time and for many individuals the monogamic system inevitably generates serious frustrations (and not merely sexual frustrations). Similarly, the system of monogamy is, I contend, the root cause of prostitution; (it is futile to try and explain such a universal phenomenon in terms of human moral frailty).

2. It ill becomes some of those with a public voice (e.g. politicians, the media) who routinely downplay the risks of ozone depletion and of nuclear power and weapons to lecture anyone on the need for safe sex. This said, there is a difference in that an appeal to individual consciences on the safe sex issue can hope to succeed, whereas there is a sense of helplessness with regard to what is, objectively speaking, the far greater potential threat to human survival arising from destruction of the environment. (Unprotected exposure to the sun's radiation, for example, could easily kill us all, without exception, if we really do destroy the ozone layer, whereas some people, and be it only a tiny minority, are, on the epidemiological evidence, always likely to develop immunity against a disease.)

3. We seem, to an extent at least, to have entered on a norm of sequential, rather than lifelong marriage. Is there anything wrong with this? And is it more or less desirable than the proposal I am making, which might be

144

described as concurrent marriage? One problem is that marriage is still intended to be permanent, and associated with this is the question of what happens when the relationship ends. Usually we cope reasonably well with the idea that we may drift apart from our friends, and there need be no rancour in this process; it is accepted as being just part of life. A loose acquaintance may well continue. The situation is somewhat different when lovers part, and radically different when notice is given to a long-term intimate relationship. Now there is a rupture which inevitably weighs on us more than any mere drifting apart.

One argument for concurrent marriage is that it actually allows breaks to be relatively gentle while at the same time making them less necessary. Sequential marriage does not normally allow for such gentleness. One reason is that a significant dependency has been generated in the name of a projected permanence, and abandonment under such circumstances is a serious matter, easily giving rise to bitterness. Another is that marriage involves possession, hence possessiveness and then the jealousy generated by the suspicion or sense of being dispossessed. Not infrequently, the result is that the people we have been closest to go away for ever, we are left wholly ignorant of what has become of them, and there is no prospect of renewing the friendship even at a less intense level. This is hardly the stuff of a wholesome ethics.

4. See my "Personhood and Eroticism" for a development of this point.

For an alternative formulation of these issues, see my "Against Couples", originally published in the Journal of Applied Philosophy, Vol. 1, No. 2, 1984, and reprinted in *Applied Philosophy: Morals and Metaphysics in Contemporary Debate*, Edited by Brenda Almond and Donald Hill (Routledge, 1991)

Bibliography

Pertinent discussion of related issues may be found in my:

"Personhood and Eroticism", published in *Philosophy Now*, No. 5, Spring 1993.
"Love and Personal Relationships", forthcoming in *An Introduction to Applied Ethics*, edited by Brenda Almond (Blackwell).

"The Two Sides of Love", published in *The Journal of Applied Philosophy*, Vol. 3, No. 2, 1986

10 Prolegomenon for a critique of marriage

Bob Brecher

> I thought I saw two people coming down the road; but it was only a man and his wife.
>
> - Russian proverb[1]

The institution of marriage - "the most universal and most effective means of social control" (Comer, 1974, p. 225) - is enjoying something of a renaissance. When once a feminist's getting married would be recognised as at the very least politically problematic, it is now subsumed into the morass of personal fulfilment, individual choice and the rest of the clichés of today's postmodern liberalism; and when once gay and lesbian activists argued for "marriage for none", many are now fighting for "marriage for all". Yet the issue of marriage has attracted little explicitly philosophical attention of late, despite its interest for sociologists, anthropologists, lawyers, historians and, of course, politicians [2] Insofar as such attention cannot but give rise to the possibility of making political and moral judgements, this should perhaps be unsurprising; for to make such judgements is, in these new, "postmoral" times, all but anathema. Furthermore, the traditional liberal distinction between "private" and "public" - which marriage itself serves to entrench - makes discussion even more problematic, so that to attack marriage is all too easily construed as an unwarranted attack on particular married individuals, not least on those with whom one is attempting to conduct a debate. Disconcertingly often, even feminists, who of all the protagonists in the debate ought to know better, conflate "the personal" - which is of course political - with what might genuinely be personal to a particular person - which is quite another matter. Nothwithstanding fashionably postmodern aversion to the thought, it is indeed the case that "the personal is political"; and that is why it is not at all a *personal* matter.

147

What follows, then, is a sketch for the beginnings of a critique of the institution of marriage, indicating something of the structure in which such a critique might be framed and suggesting what might be central to its content. I shall argue that marriage is politically important and no more neutral than is, say, the British State, and suggest that while the Right knows this perfectly well, the Left does not, should do, and will remain intellectually and politically hampered until this despairing delusion is remedied. (I develop this latter argument elsewhere, in a broader context [3].)

It is hardly controversial to look to *use* in order to discover meaning. To what use, one might therefore ask, is the institution of marriage put? Clearly, different groups of people - members of different religious communities most obviously - would give different answers. But my question is not a semi-sociological one. So I simply put on one side issues to do with how the term is understood and what the institution means in the context of specific self-identified groups. (It is worth noting, though, that the more specific the groups - Catholics rather than Christians; Orthodox Jews rather than just Jews; perhaps even certain groups of British muslims rather than Muslim Britons - the more explicit the role of marriage within the particular vision of society in terms of which that group identifies itself, and thus the more explicit its meaning.) My target is simply the secular institution at its barest and at its greatest distance from any such specificities - namely as expressed at its ideological blandest by a marriage contracted in a Register Office. But it would be a mistake to suppose that ideological blandness and absence of ideology are one and the same. And the fundamental point of the ideology at work can be summed up in one word: ownership - by men, of women. Again, I am talking about meaning and use - not about the good intentions, nor even the explicit efforts, of individuals. As an institution, marriage both expresses and endorses men's ownership of women. In practice, of course, women are often permitted to "own" *in the domestic sphere* only the husbands who therein offer them protection from the public world in return for their own absence from that world - the public sphere in which men own their wives, and, by extension, men own women.[4] Secularisation notwithstanding, St. Paul's is still the classic, if often unspoken, view:

(Even so) husbands should love their wives as their own bodies. He who loves his wife loves himself... (however) let each one of you love his wife as himself, and let the wife see that she respects her husband (Eph. 5, 28-30).

Marriage as ownership

In the Spring of 1994, the University of Central Lancashire decided that it would no longer be acceptable for its employees to introduce people as "my wife" or "my husband", a decision which was the occasion of much mockery of its so-called "political correctness". Those who object would presumably deny that the term "my" implies ownership here, and that "my wife" is significantly, as well as grammatically, indistinguishable from "my friend"; or that "my husband" weighs against "my wife" sufficiently to suggest a mutuality which would defuse my charge that marriage institutionalizes the ownership by men of women.

Suppose that I am entirely mistaken about marriage as serving to assist in the institutionalization of ownership and as expressing one, crucial, instance of such institutionalization. In that case, if marriage is not the ownership by one person of another, then it is either a non-coercive contract between two individuals, along the lines of Locke's view; an expression of his "pure" liberal individualism, according to which "every Man has a *Property* in his own *Person*" (Locke, 1967, p. 27); or it is something along the lines of Hegel's "organic" analysis, according to which "its objective origin is the free consent of the persons concerned, and in particular their consent to *constitute a single person* and to give up their natural and individual personalities within this union" (Wood, 1991, p. 201, sec. 162: see also secs. 163-9) and "a contract of incorporation into a *single, unified* body" (Trainor, 1992, p. 142). The second option need not detain us, however, since it affords what is perhaps an unusual opportunity properly to invoke an *ad hominem* argument: namely that Marie von Tüchner, whom Hegel married in 1812, remains unacknowledged as organico-co-author of his work from that date onwards.

The first option seems at least more realistic. Kant famously argued that marriage was an agreement between two people for the "reciprocal use of each other's sexual organs" (Kant, 1887, p. 45) [5]: and I think he was right in supposing that it was at least that. But how could such a contract fail to be coercive in current conditions? That, of course, is the force of Carol Pateman's arguments in *The Sexual Contract (1988)*. In respect of the marriage contract, women are always the subordinate party, just as workers are in respect of employment contracts; just as workers do not sign contracts with employers on an equal footing, since the employer determines not only the terms of the contract but the very status of the parties to it, so the social structure determines the meaning of *the individual* in terms of which the two individuals concerned sign a marriage contract. And that structure is suffused with male control. An ungendered "individual" is merely a fanciful abstraction from individual women and individual men. Furthermore, "the "individual" as owner is the fulcrum on which modern patriarchy turns". (ibid., p. 14). To argue that to contract a marriage is simply a possibility which may be freely chosen or rejected by any individual, women no less than men, is no more realistic than to argue that the terms governing the sexual services offered by a prostitute and accepted by a man are freely accepted or rejected; or that the terms governing the employment of university employees are proposed and accepted by equals. Some on the political Right, of course, deny this: an individual is significantly, and responsibly, an individual whatever the circumstances and valid contracts are by definition between equals. But if this were in fact the case, then, for example, a peasant from Turkey or India who sold one of their kidneys for transplant at a price they found acceptable would be engaging in a perfectly acceptable transaction and that, I take it, constitutes a *reductio ad absurdum* of the position, as I have argued elsewhere [6]. Again as Pateman insists, "only the postulate of natural equality prevents all the stories about social contracts from turning into a variety of coercive arrangements" (ibid., p. 60). J. S. Mill's laudable but nevertheless inadequate liberalism notwithstanding, "the equality of married persons before the law" is merely an unrealised, necessary though insufficient, condition of "rendering the daily life of mankind, in any high sense, a school of moral cultivation" (Mill, 1989b, p. 159). "That best kind of equality" (ibid., p. 211) which might exist in an ideal marriage may be desirable, but it is uninstantiable. Individuals cannot escape their social, cultural, intellectual, emotional, historical and economic circumstances by some force of quasi-Nietzschean will, so as to make of their marriage - unlike others' - "a school of sympathy in equality, of living together in love, without power on one side or obedience on the other" (ibid., p. 161).

"Marriage," as Lévi-Strauss put it, "is the archetype of exchange", in which what is exchanged is "that most precious category of goods, women" (Lévi-Strauss, 1969, pp. 483, 61) [7]: and it is also the case that "women are exchanged just as words are exchanged, and, like words, women are signs" (Pateman, 1988, p. 60). This is not, of course, to deny that men too are signs: the point, however, is that very little is what it is and not another thing too. Lee Comer's statement of the position, offered some twenty years ago, has not been bettered:

> Marriage is the first and basic model of the division of labour and power between the sexes, the legalized sanction whereby society justifies the public separation of men from women by throwing them together in private. Within the institution of marriage, men and women are supposed to resolve the conflicts of the public domain, where the power, education and money are so massively weighted in favour of men...Without marriage as the private safety valve for public conflict,

women would not tolerate the injustices of unequal pay, power and education and the degradation of sexual objectification - all the things, in fact, which make up the sum total of their usefulness...Marriage does not solve these conflicts but the fact that it contains them is what makes it such an effective and useful form of social control (Comer, 1974, p. 229).

But is this not just a luridly prejudiced interpretation of the institution? After all, marriage might have a bleak history, as does so much else; and there are doubtless many unreconstructed individuals whose explicit intentions remain firmly rooted in that history; in today's circumstances, however, far from marriage being inimical to any agenda for liberation, it "is the natural antidote to the phenomenon referred to in modern times as alienation" (Hoshii, 1986, p. 6). But the following description Lee Comer herself gave of the conditions of married life only twenty years ago have changed radically (ibid., p. 68):

The pious statements of the pundits and sociologists on the equal status of women in marriage is revealed for the nonsense it is in a system where a woman cannot prosecute her husband for rape;

now, at last and despite efforts to resist the notion of marital rape, she can.

A woman pays the rates out of her own earnings and the receipt is sent to her husband;

this is no longer the unchallenged norm.

Her earnings for income tax purposes are added to her husband's so that he knows how much she earns but she has no right to know what he earns;

no longer so.

Her income tax rebates are paid to her husband;

not since income tax has come to be assessed individually.

A woman must have her husband's permission to have a contraceptive device fitted into her womb or to be sterilised;

not any more. The same goes for tax relief for a dependent husband and other financial arrangements such as those concerning mortgages and hire purchase agreements, the constitution of juries, and the recent phasing out of "family" passports. Simone de Beauvoir's claim, made in the late 40s, that "Economic evolution in women's situation is in process of upsetting the institution of marriage" (de Beauvoir, 1989, p. 425) appears to be largely vindicated. Certainly it would be absurd to deny the scope and scale of the real advances that have been made in the last twenty years or so. Why then does marriage not provide just that haven, that antidote to alienation, that its defenders claim on its behalf?

Well, in certain individual instances, maybe it does. Much the same might be said in respect of certain individual cases alone across a whole gamut of institutions. From the mass entertainment of TV to religion: both are for some people a place of escape, a much needed opiate. But that is not what is at issue in any of these cases. For what marriage means, just as what surrogacy means, or what soap opera means, is not simply, perhaps not even at all, the sum of the intentions of those concerned. Just like all these other institutions, it cannot but have a public meaning, quite irrespective of the identity of specific individuals and their intentions. Marriage is, after all, a public contract. Thus, even if it were the case that, to quote Bertrand Russell's unintentionally ironic homily, "the essence of a good marriage is respect for each other's personality combined with that deep intimacy, physical, mental, and spiritual, which makes a serious love between man and woman the most fructifying of all human experiences" (Russell, 1961, p. 158) this would not imply that its public meaning was not, could not be, entirely inimical to it. The intentions and characters of individuals do not determine the public meaning of their actions. Not all employers - not even any employers - have to be moral monsters for it to be the case that capitalism is exploitative. In the same way, it is entirely conceivable that all those contracting a marriage might do so on a Millian or Russellian basis, and yet what that marriage was would still not be what it was "for them". For,

> any glance round society reveals that the sexes are placed on opposite poles with an enormous chasm of oppression, degradation and misunderstanding generated to keep them apart. Out of this, marriage plucks one woman and one man, ties them together with "love" and asserts that they shall live for the rest of their lives, bridge that chasm with a mixture of betrayal, sex, affection, deceit and illusion (Comer, 1974, p. 227).

To take another example: not everyone - nor even anyone - seeking a surrogate child-bearer need be selfish or uncaring of the impact of their success on the social institutionalisation of surrogacy arrangements, which in turn would have an impact on society at large - and one of which they themselves might well disapprove. People's attempted justifications of the use of medical sex-selection techniques are generally based on their own genuine desire for what they take to be a "balanced family" (the parents of three boys who want a girl) or on their own genuine conviction that theirs is no more reprehensible a way of making money than what many others do (the doctors): but neither party can (in one sense, at least) ignore the social impact of their getting what they want, whether or not they welcome the likelihood of women coming increasingly to be respected and valued as their numbers in comparison to men decrease (as those selling sex-selection services have been known to claim, apparently in all seriousness). The meaning of the institution of marriage is no exception. Again to invoke Pateman, the "final victory of contract over status is not the end of patriarchy, but the consolidation of (its) modern form" (op.cit., p. 187)

> Given the nature of the individual and the meaning of contract... this can only mean a contract between two people who own their own bodies and agree to mutual sexual use. Sexual relations then take the form of universal prostitution, marking the political defeat of women **as women**.[8]

That constitutes, to say the least, a considerable harm. Nor is it one which can be avoided on the basis of personal integrity or sincerity, simply because what it is for a woman to be a wife and what it is for a man to be a husband are not equivalent. It is not for nothing that "the ceremony will conclude with the Superintendent Registrar declaring you to be *man and wife*" (E Sussex County Council, no date given, my emphasis) [9]. Just as employment contracts imply workers' obedience to employers without explicitly specifying it, "enlightened" employers' practices notwithstanding; so a woman, in agreeing to be a wife, signals obedience to a patriarchal structure whether or not to a particular man.

In the absence of satisfactory accounts to the contrary, I conclude that it is indeed ownership which constitutes the central thrust of marriage, in respect specifically of women being owned by men. Furthermore, as I shall shortly go on to argue, marriage also furthers a social ideology of ownership quite generally.

I have taken it for granted, of course, that one person's owning another is not a good thing. But I do not think that my unwillingness to consider here such arguments as there may be to the contrary is unreasonable; and I would be interested to hear from readers who think that there are in fact any such arguments available. What I have not done in this section, however, is to show conclusively that marriage *must* constitute ownership; I have done no more than to offer an outline sketch of an argument. But even if that sketch is unconvincing as it stands - because it appears somewhat exaggerated, perhaps - there remains a set of considerations relating to the wider impact of the institution. Indeed, it is the morality-affecting aspect of institutions in general which I would wish to emphasise; and my outline treatment of its relation to ownership should be understood in that light. Yet it is not the furtherance of an ideology of ownership which alone constitutes what is wrong with the institution of marriage: rather, it is its effect on our moral thinking and practice in general which is the most important objection to it.

Morality-affecting harms

Before considering particular examples of what I have in mind, however, I need to explain the notion of morality-affecting harms.

Some concepts, then, and this is most readily recognizable in the case of newer ones, such as, for instance, "racism" or "sexism", are what I term "morality-affecting". And this is because actions, practices and events issue not only in direct consequences for specific individuals or groups, but may also affect the moral and related attitudes of people - the moral climate within which such consequences are recognized. Thus among the consequences of the Race Relations Act is the fact that some people have come to regard racism as a real harm who had not previously done so. Or consider slavery: just what is wrong with it? The classical liberal's objection to a person's voluntarily selling themselves into slavery (other things being equal of course, and the wants of no party involved being adversely affected - a not at all unimaginable scenario) is basically that, to quote Mill, "by selling himself for a slave (a man) abdicates his liberty; he forgoes any future use of it beyond that single act. He therefore defeats, in his own case, the very purpose which is the justification of allowing him to dispose of himself..."(Mill, 1989a, p. 103 [10]). But there are at least *prima facie* grounds against even the "well-regulated", one-off deal which Mill's argument fails to address. Regardless of the specific conditions of sale, and regardless of the intensity of the parties' wants, slavery is wrong. Why? Well, in very rough outline, the mere possibility of one person's owning another might well encourage the prevalence of certain sets of relations; certain sorts of use to be made by people of each other; certain further harms to come into being (the full use, according to the owner's wishes, of the slave, for example) and so on. As a practice comes to be accepted, so it becomes acceptable and where this is a morally wrong state of affairs, the harm done in engaging in the practice is one which is morality-affecting, since its having become acceptable constitutes a moral change. The harm done in owning a slave is not just that which accrues to the slave; but rather the practice of slave-owning itself has further consequences which affect what is taken to be morally right and wrong. In the same sort of way - though in a different direction - the legal reforms of the 1960s regarding male homosexuality not only made enormous differences to individual men, but also influenced the moral climate, helping to make homosexuality more acceptable. Whether or not one agrees with the substance of Hart's liberal position, Devlin's conservatism was prescient in a way liberalism tends to miss. To put it briefly, what we do in relation to such institutions makes a difference not only to those directly involved but, what is of even greater moral and political consequence, to the terms in which we then come to understand the wider issues involved. And marriage is one such institution.

Marriage as a morality-affecting harm

I shall confine my remarks to two issues, the ramifications of which, however, are very broad: first, its militating against friendship; and, second, its role as an engine of consumerism.

An argument frequently offered in favour of marriage is that it constitutes a central form of friendship, perhaps the only possible form of intimacy and security which is available in today's increasingly fragmented and alienating social circumstances and structures.[11] It is said to provide a structure within which the single most important element of human life can flourish: love. Shulamith Firestone, no defender of marriage of course, sums up the position in an admirably forthright and unabashedly realistic fashion: "contrary to popular opinion, love is not altruistic...(but) the height of selfishness" (Firestone, 1984, p. 122). Thus it requires the "containment" which marriage affords: because "the self attempts to enrich itself through the absorption of another being...it is a situation of total emotional vulnerability...(and therefore) must be not only the incorporation of the other, but an *exchange* of selves (since) anything short of a mutual exchange will hurt one or the other party..." (ibid., p. 123). Even if it does not always succeed, only marriage *can* constitute a context within which such a mutual exchange is possible.

Quite so; and so much the worse for such an exchange. The whole story about the sort of level of intimacy and dependence which we should be trying to attain should be rejected. It is its promoting just the sort of conceptions which have come to be used to justify it, and just such conceptions of their value, which is precisely what makes that social relation so harmful. For friendship thus understood - as an intimacy which excludes others - is inimical to friendliness. Consider the felt perception of friends who, sharing some intimacy, are seen as "as good as" married: the ideology of marriage determines how those are seen who are not married, who might even be making great efforts to refrain from behaving as if married. But the assumptions on which this is predicated are at best unexamined, and certainly unargued. Again, Lee Comer puts the point succinctly:

> "Real" love is only that which is exclusively focused on one person of the opposite sex - all else is labelled 'liking'. Like so much butter, romantic love must be spread thickly on one slice of bread; to spread it over several is to spread it "thinly"... A man loves God but does he love his wife less because of it? A woman loves her children. Must she love their father less? Is the tenderness I feel towards a friend's suffering of a different order than the tenderness I feel for my lover? (op. cit., pp. 219-220)

Sexual closeness to one person precludes such - and other - closeness to other people. Sexuality, and all that goes with it - intimacy, trust, interdependence - are literally, privatized. The possibility of any sort of non-familial community is excluded, and, with that, so is sexual friendship. In the classically paradoxical fashion in which ideology works, the self-fulfilment allegedly offered by romantic love in an increasingly individualistic world - the reason why it has come to replace familial economics as the putative justification of marriage - in fact serves to militate against just that which it is presented as protecting and furthering. "Self-fulfilment" is no improvement on patriarchal economic considerations: indeed, inasmuch as it obscures the reality of the situation, it is just the opposite. And while the real attractions of romantic love, and with it, of marriage, might *excuse*, they do not *justify*, any more than do those of share-buying, keeping silent or other far more serious examples of collaboration. Those who wish to justify rather than excuse must justify the ends marriage serves, rather than inventing spurious and deluded excuses masquerading as such. Again, The Right is far clearer about this than The Left. As with the greater clarity afforded by the institution of arranged marriages, which at least does not obscure its own logic, so with genuine conviction about the desirability of a society based on "Kinder, Kirche, Küche", or of one rooted in a Hobbesian "state of nature". At least we know where we are, what picture of the Good Society is being postulated when it is advocated explicitly.

Marriage brings to its concern with the "private" a particular conception and understanding of "private": it thus helps define both "private" and "public", in ways which exclude altruistic co-operation on a broader scale as a possible way of life; and in doing so excludes women yet further from even such an aetiolated conception of the public world as is permitted by that exclusion. That is to say, not only does marriage help as a matter of fact to exclude women from the public - the social and political - world, but, more insidiously, it helps define what is to count as that world: the business part of life, as Mill might have said. Whatever its actual origins, marriage is not an exchange, but the creation of a social relation. It is perhaps origin of, inevitably mirrors, and certainly supports, wage-slavery.[12] It "does not solve (these) conflicts, but the fact that it contains them is what makes it such an effective and useful form of social control" (Comer, 1974, pp. 226-7).

It is a commonplace that the capitalist market increasingly requires "flexibility" and "mobility" of its workers, a requirement of which today's individual, and more and more often part-time, contracts are but the latest example. Thus the larger groupings represented by more traditional extended family structures have to be undermined; and the nuclear family, based on a unit of two, comes to be idolised. From the point of view of those who exercise power, more than two is too communal to be sufficiently flexible and uncaring; one, however, lacking immediate close responsibilities, may be less easily cowed. Marriage thus becomes the engine of capitalist consumption, a consumption process curiously based on a particular distinction between public and private, itself based in turn on the "individual" of the empiricist tradition which made it possible for capitalism to develop. From the point of view of those upon whom it is exercised, the choice is between an impossibly isolated and isolating individualism and a "one-to-one" relationship. And from the standpoint of economic production - a not unimportant one - the world as it is (the world of employment, unemployment and over-employment) is justified by the use of its products in support of people's "private lives"; the privacy of these lives (the world of married life) is then justified as an escape from the rigours and demands of that - public - world, a world nevertheless necessary to support what now comes to be seen as a given, namely private consumption. This, in brief outline, is the model on which marriage serves to organise and justify competitive consumption. It fuels just that for which it is compensation, whether in respect of concrete goods or of leisure as something to be consumed.

Similar considerations could be offered in respect of other, related issues: for example the idea and practice of community, and of "care in the community" in particular, or of childhood. But I think that I have said enough, for purposes of this bare sketch, regarding friendship and capitalist consumption, to make clear the direction of argument I regard as required.

Finally, lest my position be misinterpreted, let me stress that I am not trying to suggest that demoting, or even eliminating, marriage would offer some sort of anti-capitalist panacea, along the lines of Wilhelm Reich's *The Mass Psychology of Fascism*. But while certainly not a sufficient condition of what feminists and others on the Left[13] might regard as progressive, it is nonetheless a necessary condition of it: it is one everyday way in which the personal may be understood as indeed political. The defence so often offered of marriage, by feminists and socialists no less than by others, as a private gesture of self-fulfilment and defence, is thus entirely misplaced: private gestures, however sincere, do not create the meanings of the public world. Indeed, they all too often serve to reinforce what they are intended to diminish, just because the protest is made in terms defined by those against whom the protest is intended. The meaning of a private gesture is, so to speak, unavoidably colonised and the protest turned back on the protestor. A private gesture is *only* a private, a personal, gesture; the personal is sharply distinguished from the political; and the gesture is lost, since only what is public can make any difference. The gesture, moreover, serves to reinforce the boundary between the two just because it cannot be carried over into the "real", public world.

The personal is indeed political; but the personal is not *political*.

Notes

1. Quoted by Lee Comer (1974), frontispiece.

2. The Penguin *What is to be Done About...?* series included a volume on the family, but not one on marriage. In its twenty years of existence, *Feminist Review* has carried no philosophical analysis of the institution or the concept; nor has the *Journal of Applied Philosophy* done so in its ten years, two somewhat tangential articles apart (Gregory, 1984 and Trainor, 1992). Other than Vetterling-Braggin, Elliston and English (eds), *Feminism and Philosophy* (1977) which has a section on the topic, feminist anthologies have very little directly on marriage - and even in this volume, only a minority of contributions in the section deal explicitly with marriage, rather than with issues of the family, motherhood, etc. The recent, otherwise comprehensive, *Women's Studies: A Reader* (1993) has a section on marriage and motherhood in which nearly all the papers on marriage are sociological, and anyway outnumbered by those on motherhood.

3. "Looking for the Good Life" (1993)

4. Jo Halliday has pointed out, in conversation, a telling parallel with middle managers: while they "own" the labour of those for whom they are "responsible", their labour is in turn owned by their employer, acquiescence in which arrangement is a condition of employment. See Pateman (1988) for trenchant criticism of Kant's exclusion of "women from the category of persons or individuals" (p. 171) - the basis of his argument that "if both parties to the contract acquire the same right...they are simultaneously owner and owned" (p. 170).

5. For a useful discussion of the precise scope of Kant's view see Trainor (1992), pp. 138-142.

6. "Organ Transplants: Donation or Payment?" (1993).

7. Cited by Pateman (1988), p. 59.

8. Cf. p. 110, where Pateman argues that the original contract (however metaphorically understood) was an agreement among men regarding their access to women: "In the beginning, in the state of nature, the "first" husband exercised a conjugal right over his wife, and all husbands enjoy this original political right by virtue of their masculine natures."

9. I am not at all sure about the extent to which this is a merely language-specific point. In French, for instance, 'femme' serves for both "woman" and "wife" in English, just as "Frau" does in German: there is much work to be done here. (It is of course unclear whether "man and wife" is more or less oppressive than an undifferentiable "femme" or "Frau".)

10. It is a tribute to Mill's perspicacity that he compares the situation of married women to that of slaves in *The Subjection of Women* (Mill, 1989): see pp. 129, 147-9, 169 and 196.

11. See for instance Lyla H. O'Driscoll, "On the Nature and Value of Marriage", in Vetterling-Braggin, Elliston and English (eds), pp. 249-263, and Mill and Russell as discussed in the section on marriage as ownership; and compare Lasch (1979) and Mount (1982) for convergent arguments from Left and Right respectively, a convergence which those on the Left, at least, should find disconcerting.

12. For detailed argument on this, see Pateman (1988), p. 148 ff.

13. The implication that feminists must be on The Left is not, of course, inadvertent.

14. Particular thanks are due to Pat FitzGerald and Jo Halliday, both for their comments on earlier drafts and for our many conversations on marriage and related issues.

Bibliography

Brecher, B. (1993), "Looking for the Good Life", *Radical Philosophy*, 65. pp. 42-44.

Brecher, B. (1993), "Organ Transplants: Donation or Payment?", in Gillon, R. (ed.), *Principles of Health Care Ethics*, John Wiley & Sons, Chichester.

Comer, L. (1974), *Wedlocked Women*, Feminist Books, London.

de Beauvoir, S. (1989), *The Second Sex*, Vintage Books, New York.

East Sussex County Council (no date), *Your Marriage*.

Firestone, S. (1984), *The Dialectic of Sex*, Women's Press, London.

Gregory, P. (1984), "Against Couples", *Journal of Applied Philosophy*, 1, 2. pp. 263-8.

Hoshii, I. (1986), *The World of Sex, vol.2: Sex and Marriage*, Paul Norbury Publications Ltd., Woodchurch.

Kant, I. (1887), *The Philosophy of Law*, T. & T. Clark, Edinburgh.

Lasch, C. (1979), *Haven in a Heartless World*, Basic Books, New York.

Lévi-Strauss, C. (1969, rev. ed.), *The Elementary Structures of Kinship*, Beacon Press, Boston.

Locke, J. (1967), *Two Treatises of Government: vol. II*, edited by Laslett, P., Cambridge University Press, Cambridge.

Mill, J.S. (1989a), *On Liberty and other writings*, edited by Collini, S., Cambridge University Press, Cambridge.

Mill, J.S. (1989b), *The Subjection of Women*, edited by Collini, S., Cambridge University Press, Cambridge

Mount, F. (1982), *The Subversive Family*, Cape, London.

Pateman, C. (1988), *The Sexual Contract*, Polity Press/Blackwell, Oxford.

Russell, B. (1961), *Marriage and Morals*, Allen and Unwin, London.

Trainor, B. T. (1992), "The State, Marriage and Divorce", *Journal of Applied Philosophy*, 9, 2. pp. 135-48.

Wood, A.W. (ed.), and Nisbet, H.B. (trans.) (1991): Hegel, G.W.F., *Elements of the Philosophy of Right*, Cambridge University Press, Cambridge.